Art and the Religious Impulse

BUCKNELL REVIEW
A Scholarly Journal of Letters, Arts, and Sciences

BUCKNELL REVIEW

Art and the Religious Impulse

Edited by
ERIC MICHAEL MAZUR

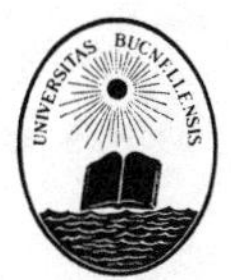

Lewisburg
Bucknell University Press
London: Associated University Presses

Associated University Presses
440 Forsgate Drive
Cranbury, NJ 08512

Associated University Presses
16 Barter Street
London WC1A 2AH, England

Associated University Presses
P.O. Box 338, Port Credit
Mississauga, Ontario
Canada L5G 4L8

The paper used in this publication meets the requirements of the
American National Standard for
Permanence of Paper for Printed Library Materials Z39.48-1984.

(Volume XLVI, Number 1)

ISBN 0-8387-5534-8
ISSN 0007-2869

Contents

Notes on Contributors   11

Introduction: A Religious Studies
     Approach to Religion and the
     Arts   ERIC MICHAEL MAZUR   15

Religion and the Arts   KATHRYN MCCLYMOND   26

How to Read a Church   PETER W. WILLIAMS   42

Textures of a Religious Life: The
     Vernacular Religious Art of Sister
     Ann Ameen   LEONARD NORMAN PRIMIANO   62

"And Art Shall Say, 'Let There Be
     Light' ": Religious Imagery and
     the Nineteenth-Century Musical
     Imagination   ANNIE JANEIRO RANDALL   84

Rebuilding Babel: Science, Fiction,
     and a New Divinity   JOHN RICKARD   91

"I'd Rather Light a Candle Than
     Curse Your Darkness": Bringing
     Religion to Light in *Raising
     Arizona*   ERIC MICHAEL MAZUR   104

The Art of Idolatry: Violent
     Expressions of the Spiritual
     in Contemporary Performance
     Art   DAWN PERLMUTTER   125

Symbolic Politics: Public Funding
     of the Arts   MATTHEW C. MOEN   141

Recent Issues of BUCKNELL REVIEW

Culture and Education in Victorian England
Classics and Cinema
Reconfiguring the Renaissance: Essays in Critical Materialism
Wordsworth in Context
Turning the Century: Feminist Theory in the 1990s
Black/White Writing: Essays on South African Literature
Worldviews and Ecology
Irishness and (Post)Modernism
Anthropology and the German Enlightenment: Perspectives on Humanity
*Having Our Way: Women Rewriting Tradition in Twentieth-Century
    America*
Self-Conscious Art: A Tribute to John W. Kronik
Sound and Light: La Monte Young/Marian Zazeela
Perspectives on Contemporary Spanish American Theatre
Reviewing Orpheus: Essays on the Cinema and Art of Jean Cocteau
Questioning History: The Postmodern Turn to the Eighteenth Century
Making History: Textuality and the Forms of Eighteenth-Century Culture
History and Memory: Suffering and Art
Rites of Passage in Ancient Greece: Literature, Religion, Society
Bakhtin and the Nation
New Essays in Ecofeminist Literary Criticism
Caribbean Cultural Identities
Lorca, Buñuel, Dalí: Art and Theory
Untrodden Regions of the Mind: Romanticism and Psychoanalysis

Acknowledgments

The material that would become this volume began as a series of lunch-time presentations in the Spring semester, 1998, for the semester-long "Religious Studies Forum" under the auspices of the Department of Religion at Bucknell University. I would like to thank my colleagues in that department for helping me to conceptualize the initial forum, the department secretary, Stephanie Snyder, for helping me with the logistics, and the original presenters of that forum for their willingness to participate.

I would also like to thank Pauline Fletcher for her assistance in bringing these essays together for the *Bucknell Review* and, of course, the contributors to this volume for their patience and generosity.

Of greatest importance to me, however, has been the support and assistance I have received from my wife, Claudia. I dedicate this volume to her; she has brought both religion and art into my life, and I will be forever grateful.

Notes on Contributors

ERIC MICHAEL MAZUR is an assistant professor of religion at Bucknell University, where he teaches in the area of religion and American culture. He is the author of *The Americanization of Religious Minorities: Confronting the Constitutional Order* (1999), and co-editor of *God in the Details: American Religion in Popular Culture* (2000) as well as articles on the sociology of American religion and Native American legal disputes over religion.

KATHRYN MCCLYMOND is an assistant professor at Georgia State University (Atlanta). She teaches and conducts research as a comparative historian of religions, working particularly in Jewish and Hindu traditions of sacrifice, and also has a secondary specialization in religion and literature. Current projects include "The Gospel According to Oprah," an examination of how Oprah Winfrey has established a canon of fiction that teaches specific societal values (via a particular literary style) for a large segment of American society.

MATTHEW C. MOEN is a professor of political science at the University of Maine. He has published numerous articles and four books on American national politics, including *The Christian Right and Congress* (1989), *The Transformation of the Christian Right* (1992), and *The Contemporary Congress: A Bicameral Approach* (1998). He was named University of Maine Trustee Professor for 2000–2001.

DAWN PERLMUTTER is an associate professor of art and philosophy at Cheyney University of Pennsylvania. She teaches courses in ethics, aesthetics, cultural studies, contemporary moral issues and alternative religions, and is the editor and an author of *Reclaiming the Spiritual in Art* (1999). She is currently working on a forthcoming book titled *Blood Rituals: Investigating Occult Crime.*

LEONARD NORMAN PRIMIANO is an associate professor of religious studies at Cabrini College, Radnor, Pennsylvania. He is the author of a forthcoming book on "Dignity," an American Catholic gay and lesbian religious group, and producer and writer of a documentary, *I Know You Are God: The Marriage of Father and Mother Divine,* which examines Father Divine's International Peace Mission Movement (in production). He was a consultant on folk and popular religion for the touring exhibition, "Angels from the Vatican: The Invisible Made Visible."

ANNIE JANEIRO RANDALL is an associate professor of musicology at Bucknell University. Her principal areas of research are late eighteenth-century Weimar, Puccini's late operas, and the music of political resistance.

JOHN RICKARD teaches English at Bucknell University, where he is the NEH Chair in the Humanities. He has published essays on James Joyce and other Irish writers and is the editor of *Irishness and (Post)-Modernism* (*Bucknell Review* 38.1, 1994) and the author of *Joyce's Book of Memory: The Mnemotechnic of "Ulysses"* (1998).

PETER W. WILLIAMS is Distinguished Professor of Comparative Religion and American Studies at Miami University (Oxford, Ohio). He is the author of numerous articles and books on religion in America, including *Houses of God: Region, Religion, and Architecture in the United States* (1997), *America's Religions: Traditions and Cultures* (1996), and *Popular Religion in America: Symbolic Change and the Modernization Process in Historical Perspective* (1989). He is also an editor of *Perspectives on American Religion and Culture: A Reader* (1999).

BUCKNELL REVIEW

Art and the Religious Impulse

Introduction: A Religious Studies Approach to Religion and the Arts

> What is to become "our world" must first be "created," and every creation has a paradigmatic model—the creation of the universe by the gods.
>
> —Mircea Eliade

IN the beginning, God created . . ." With these opening words, the sacred scriptures of both Judaism and Christianity proclaim the relationship between divinity and creativity. The first act of the deity is a creative one—God creates—and from that action the entirety of the cosmos comes into being. Indeed, this relationship is not limited simply to these two religious traditions: note David and Margaret Leeming, "virtually all cultures have creation myths." Each of these myths, which provides their respective cultures with a "sense of its particular identity," also serves as "a symbolic model for the society's way of life, its world view." As Leeming and Leeming conclude, this model manifests itself in a variety of ways within a society, including in its "ritual, culture heroes, ethics, and even art and architecture."[1]

Though it is likely that the Leemings add the "even" before "art and architecture" only to suggest the range of a religious worldview's impact on a culture, we should be careful not to be cavalier when we examine the relationship between religion and art. The Leemings themselves compare the role of the creation myth to the artistic impulse in the painter or poet as they explain how the process of retelling the creation myth works within a culture. Creation myths enable societies to see themselves "in relation to the cosmos," and the basic stories generally follow a similar pattern regarding "the process by which chaos becomes cosmos, no-thing becomes some-thing." They argue that the telling of creation myths (along with other religious myths), "like painting, singing, dancing, love-making, and eating," is therefore not only a form of recreation, but also a process of re-creation, of orientation and renewal, and a desire to make meaning in the face of meaninglessness. "In short," they conclude, "the archetype of the creation myth speaks to the equally universal drive for differentiation from nothingness that is expressed by everything that exists in the universe.[2] Scholar of art and religion Diane Apostolos-Cappadona may put it a bit more accurately when she writes:

> As the visualization of experiences, stories and aspirations, art translates into perceptible imagery what it means to be human, while religion, as the spiritual inspiration for human creativity and culture, binds together humanity and divinity through ritual and myth.[3]

In this dance of experience, representation and meaning, art and religion form their powerful bond.

But only the person who has never really *experienced* art or religion beyond the cognitive realm would suggest that any process of meaning-construction functions solely on the cognitive level (and to be sure, this is *not* what the Leemings or Apostolos-Cappadona suggest). Apostolos-Cappadona herself refers to phenomenologist of religion Rudolf Otto, who explores the experiential, nonrational aspect of religion. In his classic work, *The Idea of the Holy*, Otto argues that a true religious experience is beyond description and that it evokes in the believer feelings of dependence, insignificance, and fear, while at the same time eliciting feelings of love, wonder, and fascination. He identifies this as an experience of the numinous (from the Latin *numen*, "divine will"), and suggests that art (among other aspects of human existence) facilitates these experiences. He argues that art has "a means of creating a unique impression"— which he calls magical—that is "nothing but a suppressed and dimmed form of the numinous." He suggests that, as art becomes great art, "the point is reached at which we may no longer speak of the 'magical,' but rather are confronted with the numinous itself, with all its impelling motive power, transcending reason, expressed in sweeping lines and rhythms."[4] As Apostolos-Cappadona puts it: "By its intrinsic and natural relationship to truth and beauty and to human sensibilities, art may evoke a religious experience."[5]

Religion scholar Mircea Eliade takes this one step further by noting that in terms of religion, art (which he identifies as "sacred art")[6] seeks "to represent the invisible by means of the visible," by translating "religious experience and a metaphysical conception of the world and of human existence into a concrete, representational form." A central element in this translation, however, is the involvement of the deity, who participates "by revealing himself to man and allowing himself to be perceived in form or figure." The key is not simply those feelings the believer might be having, but the experience of engagement between the believer and the deity. As Eliade concludes: "Every religious expression in art represents . . . an encounter between man and the divine."[7]

It is this involvement of the divinity that reinforces the relationship between religion and art, makes them enterprises of greater significance than the sum of their parts, and thus highlights our need to exercise care when drawing connections between the two. Humans engage in creative acts at any given moment, but when those acts involve a transcendent referent, they become cosmically significant. If we connect religious significance to meaning-construction and not location, could not any work of art be religious? Or must we follow the trend of some scholars of religion and distinguish between art that is religious and art that is secular?[8] We tread on thin ice if we pursue this line too far, for certainly there must be a way of distinguishing religious and nonreligious art? Even Otto notes that in no form is art "more than an 'indirect' means of representing the numinous."[9] But as Eliade quotes from fourteenth-century Catholic theologian William of Ockham: "It is an article of the [Christian] Faith that God took on the nature of a human being. By this same token He can take on that of a stone or of a piece of wood."[10] As contemporary scholars have come to recognize that religion (or the religious impulse) occupies more than the institutions built up around it, it becomes more important to look to all aspects of human experience to find it.

The following collection of articles in this issue of the *Bucknell Review* examines the relationship between religion and art in its variety of manifestations. On the most basic level, the various essays attempt to address this relationship by examining different art forms, including the visual arts (performing and film), music, literature, architecture, folk art, as well as the political debates surrounding the public funding of art in the United States. However, these essays have not been chosen simply to "cover the waterfront," but to follow the logic of Otto and Eliade illustrated above; namely, that 1) there is a profound relationship between religion and art because 2) both serve as meaning-constructing and orientation processes providing believers with the ability to imagine and experience (if not understand) transcendence.

However, these two principles must be filtered through contemporary arguments concerning religious organization, particularly in the modern (or even postmodern) West. Though there has been tension between institutional structures and anti-institutional forces since the beginnings of human organization, this has certainly been a religious leitmotif of the Western world since the Protestant Reformation. With a rise in globalism and an expansion of communication and information technology, traditional religious institutions continue to face a challenge to their presumed historic monopolization of meaning-construction and maintenance. This is not to say, however, that the church, synagogue, and mosque are insignificant, but simply that they are not the sole providers of the types of orientation and (though we must now use the word hesitantly) spirituality that traditionally have been found in religious organizations and institutions. This being the case, religiosity (or the religious impulse) can be found in a variety of human endeavors that might once have seemed nontraditional, anti-institutional, or even nonreligious.[11] As more work in the discipline continues to show, the future of the academic study of religion might no longer be pursued exclusively from an institutional viewpoint but from viewpoints that include noninstitutional, individual, and functionally equivalent aspects of religion.

Responding to the Nietzschean "death of God" philosophy that was increasingly powerful throughout the twentieth century, Eliade argues that what he calls "religious art" has not been produced "for more than a century." But, he continues, this is not to say that "the 'sacred' has completely disappeared in modern art." Instead, he suggests that

> it has become *unrecognizable*; it is camouflaged in forms, purposes and meanings which are apparently "profane." The sacred is not *obvious*, as it was for example in the art of the Middle Ages. One does not recognize it *immediately* and *easily*, because it is no longer expressed in a conventional religious language.[12]

Not surprisingly, in a discussion of the location of the sacred in contemporary society, sociologist of religion Phillip Hammond makes the same argument, suggesting that despite arguments regarding the secularization of society, the sacred was not lost, but needed to be found using a differently focused lens.[13]

Art, as an aspect of human existence with so close a relationship to religion, is one such lens through which we can find religion. In the first essay, Kathryn McClymond provides an introduction to the relationship between religion and the arts, as well as a basic understanding of how to grapple with such broad aspects of human existence. Distinguishing between the practice and the study of religion, McClymond observes the different roles played by the arts in the religious world. In terms of the practice of religion, the arts can serve the needs of specific members or whole communities of adherents, "either reinforcing or challenging the community's views" through education, worship, or the introduction of unorthodox ideas or interpretations. In the study of religion, the arts can serve as a way for an outsider (or even a member) to gain a new understanding of the religious individual or community, and "present new information and insights to those encountering a particular religious community." However, even with these two functions, there is still room for conflict in the relationship, and McClymond suggests that as the world moves into the twenty-first century, both technology (particularly in relation to the computer) and pluralism will have a profound impact on the relationship between religion and the arts, from the dissemination of images across the Internet to the mixing and blending of religious imagery in increasingly diverse cultures. McClymond suggests that, as the consensus dissipates over how different segments of society define both art and religion, the relationship between the two will only continue to diverge, creating greater challenges for each other.

Before pursuing this further, however, those areas in which religion and the arts are still very much in collaboration must be considered. One logical place to begin an examination of religion and the arts in symbiosis is in the external materiality of a religious culture—in the "stuff" that fills the religious life. Peter W. Williams offers a tour of such "stuff," examining how it is that members of religious communities have used architecture in the service of religion (and sometimes vice versa) in their houses of worship. Noting that in America, churches are "one of the most abundant and ubiquitous features of the built landscape" (after homes and shops), Williams explores the effects of geography, economics, and history—in addition to theology—on the buildings used by the various religious communities in the United States. Interpreting a building's use of scale, siting, and style, he encourages the reader to see these buildings—so important to such a large and diverse population—"not just as generic icons of religiosity but rather as particular embodiments of that cultural impulse, simultaneously unique and representative." In his examination, he also provides a lexicon to make familiar the seemingly exotic, providing the reader an opportunity to tell a *narthex* from a *nave,* a *minbar* from a *mihrab,* empowering even the outsider with the ability to "read" the architecture of an unfamiliar house of worship.

As noted earlier, not all of what constitutes religion (or the religious impulse) occurs in the house of worship or even under the watchful eyes of empowered religious authorities. Leonard Norman Primiano discusses Sister Ann Ameen, a Canadian rugmaker who spent her life weaving her religious worldview and meaning system into her rag rugs. Primiano, exploring the concept of vernacular religion, writes that Ameen "combined her Protestant evangelical sensibility . . . her Christian iconophilia, her American Holiness training, her cultural knowledge as a Newfoundlander, and all the other influences on her as a religious 'American' to . . . express her encounter, her contact, her exchange of religion, and ultimately her understanding and negotiation of religion as she lived and practiced it in her everyday life." Her rugs, serving as both objects of art and devotion, were of divine inspiration and thus were able to transcend their role as an ordinarily mundane object (worthy of little consideration other than as a place to wipe one's feet) and become a tableau mating the divine and the profane world in which she lived. In addition to their monetary value (which provided funds for Ameen's missionary interests), these rugs were also part of this devout Christian's witnessing, assisting her in the evangelization of any and all viewers and enabling her to negotiate the different religious and cultural influences in her world.

Ameen's rugs, expressions of intense faith, also provide a clue to the movement of religious meaning from institutional to noninstitutional settings that have been the hallmark of religion throughout time and memory. In her essay on nineteenth-century composers and their creations, Annie Janeiro Randall examines a point beyond (but still affected by) the watershed moment of the Protestant Reformation and discusses the "crypto-religious sensibility . . . embedded in the Western European art music tradition." Exploring the prose of Richard Wagner, Franz Liszt, Carl Zelter, and Felix Mendelssohn (as well as the impact of those writings on others), Randall identifies a transition in music from its traditional religious setting (in the service of the church) to a setting of sui generis meaning and significance, where the music and its performance could be regarded as sacred without any manifestation of traditional religious institutionality. "This type of thinking," she writes, "made it quite possible for the listener to posit a divine presence at the center of the 'angelically pure art,' and to imagine a musical performance to be a religious experience." The culture, religiously released in the sixteenth century from the need to interact with the divine presence through a mediating religious institution, now had the means by which to interact with the divine presence in music. A product of the Protestant Reformation, the shift empowered a new, musical, priesthood of all listeners, as it were, and a more "protestant" experience of music. The music, to borrow from Otto, enabled the listener to personally experience the numinous unfettered by any religious institution.

John Rickard's essay leads from the nineteenth century into the present (and beyond) with his exploration of fiction and science. Starting from the Genesis story of the Tower of Babel and its lesson of punishment for humanity's hubris, Rickard explores contemporary fiction and its attitude toward "posthuman" evolution, finding the lessons it teaches much more optimistic than those learned from the biblical text or even such classic works as Mary Shelley's *Frankenstein*. He notes that these new works suggest that "human beings can or even should embrace technology and the technologization of the human body in an attempt to evolve self-consciously into a new species." Referring to the "death of God" theology prominent in the modern world, Rickard argues that this new literature leaves no conclusion but that such control would make the human race "a new divinity, to move into the gap opened by the death of the old divinity." These writers, as Rickard chronicles, conclude that "we are indeed rebuilding Babel, seemingly secure in the sense that we are climbing into a vacant space waiting to be occupied and now devoid of a punishing God."

Implying not that God is dead, but that He isn't here right now, Eric Michael Mazur explores the effect of the deinstitutionalization of religion in his examination of the film *Raising Arizona*. By positing the film as a modern morality play and identifying religious elements within the film, Mazur is able to show the power of religious symbolism and narrative structure beyond the conscious design of the writers or actors. He then suggests that with changes in contemporary American religious practice (particularly with regard to reduced loyalty for institutional affiliation and a subsequent reduction in exposure to any traditional religious education), it is not surprising that such remnants of traditional religion were missed by most of the reviewing (and likely, the viewing) audience. "In contemporary America," he argues, large segments of the population have moved away from "traditional religion" as their source of "meaning-construction and maintenance." As a result, fewer people are introduced to the symbols traditionally used to communicate a culture. The result, he concludes, could be a religiously illiterate society, where people continue to use the symbols and structures of their cultural heritage even as they lose any sense of their meaning or context.

It would seem that Apostolos-Cappadona is correct, that a significant element in the relationship between religion and art is the "issue of power—social, political, and economic as well as spiritual."[14] If both are means by which meaning and orientation are explored and expressed, it should come as no surprise that there will be conflict when different meanings or orientations encounter one another. Eliade suggests that even though "the great majority of artists do not seem to have 'faith' in the traditional sense," and that they are "not consciously religious," it is still the case "that the sacred, although unrecognizable, is present in their works."[15] While we (or any number of artists) might disagree with him about how religious contemporary artists may or may not be, it does seem true that there is no easy way to separate "religious" from "nonreligious" art (if such an endeavor is even worth pursuing). It may not be that all art is *traditionally* religious; if meaning-construction, orientation, or even Otto's concept of the numinous are the benchmarks, however, it must be the case that many seemingly nonreligious (and even some seemingly antireligious) works are themselves part of the "religious" corpus.

Dawn Perlmutter explores the world of performance art—particularly in its use of the body, body parts, and body products—and argues that while these performances may at times be "intentional acts of blasphemy to provoke controversy," they are more likely to be "authentic attempts by artists to reclaim the spiritual in their lives." Perlmutter examines the close parallels between the work of several performance artists and traditional (if, in some cases, non-Western) religious practice, from Christian to Native American and Aztec cultures. She argues that in an inversion of traditional religious practice, many of these artists are performing acts that might seem to traditional (primarily Christian) believers to be idolatrous but which can also be understood to be new and transformative forms of spirituality not only for the artist but also for the audience/particpant in the performance. Using violence as a form of mortification, and sacrifice, performance art "represents a struggle between those wishing to retain the ethics and morality of a monotheistic society and those who believe in other ideologies." Perlmutter, noting that art "is a mirror that reflects the soul of American culture," concludes that "violence, self-mutilation, and the use of blood in contemporary performance art is revealing a strong need for ritual experience."

This being the case, and such violent expressions are themselves serving as venues for the religious impulse and coming to form the basis of religious meaning-construction, it is not surprising that during the last few decades in the United States as conservative Christianity has played a more prominent role in national politics, debates over issues that would not seem particularly religious are being waged as if the community of the faithful were itself under attack. As Matthew C. Moen describes it, the congressional debate over public funding of the arts has been one that focuses not only on how one defines art but over how one defines culture and where the power to make that definition normative lies. Using the "culture war" thesis made popular by sociologist James Davison Hunter, Moen explores the nature and effect of the legislative process on budget authorizations and allocations for the National Endowment for the Arts (NEA) from its founding in the mid-1960s, through the socially and fiscally conservative years of the Reagan/Bush administrations, up to the later years of the Clinton administration. By presenting the opposition to public funding of the NEA (primarily conservative Christians) as religiously driven to protect traditional mores (as opposed to politically driven to reduce federal spending), Moen explains why it has been the case that a program which has represented such a small segment of the federal budget has occupied such a prominent position in public rhetoric. As he notes, with no end in sight to the battles between traditionalists and progressives, the NEA will "enjoy a long life of ill health . . . a symbol of a cultural divide that shrinks and expands at different times, but does not go away."

Scholar of Jainism John Cort has argued that scholars "tend to go to texts as sources of information in their research" and suggests that it is only through the analysis of the totality of a culture's products that one can begin to understand it.[16] While his critique is

aimed primarily at scholars of religion, it is worthwhile for all interpreters of culture to pay heed. Particularly in the industrialized
world, where globalism, commercialism, and cultural interaction
make the *picture* of the pen mightier than the pen, it is important to
add a portion of materiality to any analysis of contemporary culture,
even (if not especially) religious culture.

Every product of material culture has, according to Nadine Pence
Frantz, three "worlds" in which it functions: the world "behind the
work" (its history), the world "of the work" (its content, form), and
the world "in front of the work" (its effect on others, either individually or socially). While each of the authors contributing to this collection has, to one degree or another, provided for the reader the
means to enter the three worlds of the particular works (or genres)
they examine, we must also put all of this into what Frantz calls the
"locative context"—the big picture, as it were.[17] What does the sum
of the data tell us about the subject?

First, as the essays by McClymond and Williams illustrate, there is
no question that the relationship between religion and the arts is
both complex and (at times) mutually beneficial.

Second, the "secularization" of religion seems to be a myth. As
discussions by Primiano, Randall, and Rickard illustrate, if we understand religion (or rather, the religious impulse) as noninstitutional,
we needn't look for it in church; we needn't even look for it in traditionally "religious" activities. However, as Mazur argues, there is a
danger that as the religious impulse becomes less institutionally
grounded, there will be a sense of cultural "jet lag" in the sense that
remnants of the old order will survive into the new order but with a
significantly different (if not vacant) function.

Third, human activities that provide meaning and orientation,
and which enable the participant (either the artist or the "audience") to transcend human, rational experience, can fill many of
the roles historically reserved for religion (if not all of them). As
Perlmutter and Moen illustrate, the arts, which provide humanity
with such opportunities, are (for some, at any rate) in competition
with traditional religious institutions. While this may not always be a
welcome reality, it does nonetheless increasingly seem to be the case.

In the end, we are left with more questions than answers. The
practice common in the West of studying religion separate from art
(as well as from many other aspects of life) seems foolhardy. While
early scholars of religion described religion (or more commonly,
the sacred) as opposed to the profane, it might be more honest to

pursue them in their conjunction rather than in their disjunction. Religion and art, both systems of meaning-construction and orientation, provide people with an opportunity to transcend the experiences of the individual and make contact—not only with other people, but with something beyond any person. As such, the study of religion and art can provide greater insight into the cultures of humanity than simply the study of one or the other.

ERIC MICHAEL MAZUR

Notes

1. David Adams Leeming and Margaret Adams Leeming, *Encyclopedia of Creation Myths* (Santa Barbara, Calif.: ABC-CLIO, 1994), vii.

2. Ibid., vii, viii.

3. Diane Apostolos-Cappadona, *Dictionary of Art*, s.v. "Religion and art."

4. Rudolf Otto, *The Idea of the Holy*, trans. John W. Harvey (New York: Oxford University Press, 1928), 69.

5. *Dictionary of Art*, s.v. "Religion and art."

6. Eliade notes: "The fact that originally all art was 'sacred' should not be allowed to obscure the distinction that has always existed between activities in which this sacred quality is merely implicit . . . and those activities designed specifically to proclaim, meditate upon, and worship a sacred power or being." Mircea Eliade, "Divinities: Art and the Divine," in *Mircea Eliade: Symbolism, the Sacred, and the Arts*, ed. Diane Apostolos-Cappadona (New York: Crossroad Publishing, 1985), 55.

7. Ibid.

8. For a definition of art and religion that seems to ignore nontradition-based art, see the *HarperCollins Dictionary of Religion*, s.v. "art and religion."

9. Otto, *The Idea of the Holy*, 70. Otto identifies several ways artists represent the numinous indirectly, including the use of silence, darkness, and emptiness; ibid., 70–73.

10. Eliade, "Divinities," 56. Eliade provides the original Latin: *Est articulus fidei quod Deus assumpsit naturam humanam. Para ratione potest assumere lapidem aut lignum.*

11. For essays exploring the manifestation of religious impulses in seemingly nonreligious venues, see Eric Michael Mazur and Kate McCarthy, eds., *God in the Details: American Religion in Popular Culture* (New York: Routledge, 2001).

12. Mircea Eliade, "The Sacred and the Modern Artist," in *Mircea Eliade: Symbolism, the Sacred, and the Arts*, 81–82.

13. Phillip Hammond, ed., *The Sacred in a Secular Age* (Berkeley: University of California Press, 1985), particularly 4–6.

14. Apostolos-Cappadona, *Dictionary of Art*, s.v. "Religion and art."

15. Eliade, "The Sacred and the Modern Artist," 82.

16. John E. Cort, "Art, Religion, and Material Culture: Some Reflections on Method," *Journal of the American Academy of Religion* 64, no. 3 (Fall 1996): 613.

17. Nadine Pence Frantz, "Material Culture, Understanding, and Meaning: Writing and Picturing," *Journal of the American Academy of Religion* 66, no. 4 (Winter 1998): 812, 801.

Religion and the Arts

Kathryn McClymond
Georgia State University

CHAIM Potok's novel *My Name Is Asher Lev* describes the life of a young Jewish painter living in New York City.[1] At a critical moment in the story Lev decides to paint a work that conveys the suffering his mother experienced during long separations from her husband when he traveled to Israel. The artist chooses to portray his mother's anguish as a kind of crucifixion:

> With charcoal, I drew the frame of the living-room window of our Brooklyn apartment. I drew the strip of the Venetian blind a few inches from the top of the window. On top—not behind this time, but on top—of the window I drew my mother in her housecoat, with her arms extended along the horizontal of the blind, her wrists tied to it with the cords of the blind, her legs tied at the ankles to the vertical of the inner frame with another section of the cord of the blind. I arched her body and twisted her head.[2]

The young Jewish artist struggles with the decision to incorporate a crucifixion in his painting, anticipating a strong negative reaction from his parents and from his community as a whole. Yet he ultimately concludes that a crucifixion is the only image with the cultural and artistic resonance to generate the visual impact he desires: "I created this painting—an observant Jew working on a crucifixion because there was no aesthetic mold in his own religious tradition into which he could pour a painting of ultimate anguish and torment."[3] As Lev fears, his parents and community are shocked by his work.

The problems Lev experiences by using the image of the crucifix reflect millennia of intimacy and conflict between religious communities and the arts. The arts—literature, drama, painting, sculpture, dance, music, and architecture—have had a tangled love-hate relationship with religion over the centuries. Particularly in the West, religious communities nurtured the arts because they served several functions within the tradition, educating devotees and facilitating worship. Yet over time, as the arts developed independently from institutional religious control and influence, art also became a vehicle for challenging religious assumptions and authority.

Within the West[4] there is a tradition of viewing the artist as a creator, much like God himself. The late jazz trombonist J. J. Johnson once remarked: "There is nothing more rewarding than making something out of nothing," alluding to a similarity between artistic and divine creativity.[5] In Western thought the artist's activity imitates God's activity at the moment of creation. The notion that artists are creators similar to God has influenced different streams of artistic interpretation. Some streams characterize the artwork as an extension of the artist, reflecting her personality and concerns. Other streams emphasize the integrity of the artwork apart from its creator, arguing that we can interpret a piece without any reference to the artist at all. Other streams focus on the social context in which a piece was created, arguing that the piece reflects its cultural setting. What is significant for our purposes is that we have a tradition of distinguishing the artwork from the artist, at least to some extent. In the same way that God is distinct from his creation, the artist stands in distinct separation from her work. The distinction between the artist and the art is significant because an artist's religious views and practices do not automatically determine the religious nature of her work. A non-Christian artist can create a piece that reflects Christian concerns.[6]

We can characterize the relationship between religion and the arts in two ways: 1) as part of the *practice* of religion, and 2) as they facilitate the *study* of religion. Many of us are aware that the study of religious traditions differs markedly from participation within religious communities. The significance of the arts depends upon the relationship one has with particular religious communities (and religion in general). In the *practice* of religion, the arts address specific religious communities or individual members of communities, either reinforcing or challenging the community's views. The arts transmit traditional stories, teach religious truths, and even question institutionally supported views. In all of these contexts the arts speak from within a specific community to an audience familiar with that community. In the *study* of religion the situation is somewhat different. The audience frequently includes those who are unfamiliar with specific religious communities. For students of religion, the arts offer multiple entrés into and expressions of a religious world that may be unfamiliar. The arts in this context do not transmit or transform previously recognized truths so much as present new information and insights to those encountering a particular religious community for the first time. The arts play significant roles in both the practice and study of religion, but in distinctly different ways.

The Arts and the Practice of Religion

Within religious communities, the arts have fulfilled various functions. They have been used to reinforce as well as to question mainstream religious ideas and practices. They have been used sympathetically to educate members about religious myths and truths and to facilitate individual and corporate worship. In addition, art has also been used as a vehicle for challenging religious institutions and authority. As a result, it is understandable that the arts have sparked strong positive and negative reactions from religious communities over the years.

The Arts and Religious Education

In the modern West we tend to think of the fine arts as distinct from religion. Many classic religious works such as the Isenheim altarpiece are currently found in museums and art galleries rather than in their original church or chapel settings.[7] But much of what we think of as art was never meant to be distinguished from religious practice at all. Rather, individual pieces were crafted as vehicles for religious instruction, teaching tools intended to communicate foundational stories and theological truths for particular religious communities. Eliot Deutsch comments: "The dominant presupposition from the Hellenistic period to the Renaissance was simply that art was subservient to . . . the demands of morality, as theologically and politically defined and understood."[8] Art, one of the material dimensions of religious life, was secondary to doctrine, the dominant dimension of religious life.

Numerous art forms contributed to the religious education of devotees. The "storytelling" arts (drama, poetry, song, and literature) originally took their subjects from religious myths. Ancient Greek dramas portrayed the lives of the gods and the great epic heroes. Christian mystery plays dramatized biblical stories and the lives of the saints.[9] Public presentations of stories fulfilled a number of important functions. They explained human and cosmic origins. They passed on important myths. They characterized certain figures as heroes and role models. They situated mundane acts on an eternal stage. In fulfilling all of these roles, storytelling in all its forms linked individuals and communities to their own religious history.

Storytelling continues to be an important element of contemporary religious experience. Dramatic presentations continue today in festival celebrations. Christmas pageants abound in most communities, for example, and annual Purim festivals include performances of the Esther story as a standard element of the celebration. While these dramatizations are often fun and raucous, they also transmit traditionally held truths about God's interactions with particular religious communities throughout history.

Dramatic performances tend to reinforce the corporate nature of religious experience. Many festival celebrations include short dramas so that children can learn their communities' stories by their parents' sides. By hearing these stories over and over, year after year, countless generations learn about the creation of the universe, the character of the divine, the nature of humanity, and the community's responsibilities in this world. The transmission of these stories becomes just as important as the stories themselves. What parent, for example, would miss her child's participation as shepherd number seven in a Christmas pageant, year after year? The event, as well as the story presented during the event, strengthens individual and family commitments to specific religious communities. Within each community, the dramatization of important stories takes on liturgical importance as opportunities for several generations to come together and to relate present experiences to a meaningful past.

Important religious stories are transmitted in a variety of forms, not just in books. Texts such as the Bible and the Torah obviously record important events and biographies, but until relatively recently many religious adherents were illiterate. In addition, until the widespread use of the printing press, written texts were largely unavailable to the community at large. Important stories had to be passed on in other ways. Even to this day, while the modern West depends on books for secular education, religious education is largely a nontextual enterprise. Stories and religious truths are communicated in other ways.

Historically, one approach was to include storytelling in public and domestic celebrations via liturgical texts, songs, and inspirational narratives. For example, the church incorporated the story of Jesus' life, death, and Resurrection in the Apostles' Creed, recited by congregants on a weekly basis. Chants and hymns frequently focused on God's attributes or the lives of Jesus and the saints, reminding parishioners of the important stories of the faith. Within Judaism the annual Pesach celebration is, in effect, a family recounting of the Exodus story, repeated from generation to generation. Family and friends gather at home around a special meal and tell the Exodus story to one another. Songs (such as the popular "Dayyenu") and games remind participants of historical examples of God's faithfulness and covenant with the Jewish people. By transmitting important stories regularly in ritual settings, community members reinforce their connection to one another and to the religious tradition as a whole.

The visual arts have also been used to provide religious instruction in various settings. Representational paintings and sculptures, for example, depict scenes from sacred stories, especially in Christianity. They portray important religious figures and episodes, using imagery rather than narrative. Church pieces such as the Ghent altarpiece have portrayed important saints and events for worshipers for centuries. Church windows (such as the western rose window of Chartres Cathedral) functioned as canvases for stained-glass artwork that captured important moments in Christian history. Certain religious historical events have been incorporated as architectural features so frequently that they can even be communicated with abstract imagery, as in Barnett Newman's *Stations of the Cross* (ca. 1960) paintings. As a result churches, including their artwork, sculpture, and architecture, functioned as grand-scale visual aids for the religious education of the masses.

Not all artwork operated on such a large scale. For example, domestic items were also used to communicate traditional stories and to illustrate religious themes in family and small group settings. Functional elements such as the Seder plate are frequently decorated to remind participants of key events in Jewish history. Nativity scenes in various forms and sizes represent the Christian birth narrative. T-shirts and jewelry with the letters "WWJD" ("What would Jesus do?"), reminding Christians to model their behavior after Jesus, have become popular in certain communities. Everyday art, as well as "fine art," has been employed to transmit sacred stories and values just as effectively as large-scale art and architecture.

It is important to note that some religious communities have traditionally been more reticent than others to incorporate representational forms in any kind of art. The use—or rejection—of representational forms to communicate religious truths reflects specific theological assumptions. For example, the early Protestant churches rejected elaborate religious art in reaction to excesses they perceived in Roman Catholic and Eastern Orthodox churches. Protestantism emphasized the preaching of the gospel, and the elevated pulpit replaced the altar as the focal point of church architecture. Icons were, for the most part, set aside. Jewish and Islamic communities usually avoid representations of God for theological reasons, but they do incorporate representations of other significant religious figures and elements. The Islamic arts, for example, include images of paradise in illuminated manuscripts, architecture, and garden design.[10]

The importance of the arts for religious education is not limited to the Western religious traditions. Classical Hindu dance, for example, recounts the stories of the gods and the ancient heroes. Most scholars trace the Hindu performing arts back to classical Sanskrit drama as outlined in the *Natyashastra* (third century B.C.E). Dramatic performances accompanied temple worship, and they included dance, music, and poetry. Today these traditions are continued in temples here in the United States, as well as in secular settings. The classic stories of the gods and heroes are communicated through specific gestures and postures that make the characters and the plot clear.

The use of the arts continues to this day and often incorporates other popular cultural phenomena. A recent Purim celebration in Boulder, Colorado, for example, incorporated characters from the popular Harry Potter children's book series in an adaptation of the story of Esther.[11] The *VeggieTales* video series uses cartoon characters to present biblical stories (with some modern twists) to young children. The performing arts, visual arts, and literature provide a kind of ongoing catechism, transmitting the foundational ideas and stories of Western religious traditions from generation to generation.

The Arts and Worship

The arts have also contributed to religious life by facilitating corporate and individual worship. Architecture plays a primary role, particularly in public worship. For example, the Temple in Jerusalem (destroyed in 70 C.E.) included a series of concentric, increasingly sacred spaces, with the Holy of Holies at the innermost core. Modern synagogues roughly parallel this layout, with the ark containing the Torah scroll at the center of the structure. Both the ancient Temple and modern synagogues architecturally represent the centrality of God in traditional Jewish life as well as his intimate presence among his chosen people. Churches, as we have mentioned, focus the congregants' attention on either the altar or the pulpit, emphasizing either the Mass or the Bible depending upon the denomination. In addition, certain churches incorporated spires, which directed the worshiper's attention to heaven, reminding him of the life to come. Islamic mosques include an arch *(mihrab)* that orients the congregation toward Mecca while praying, the most significant activity performed in a mosque. Even the seemingly "empty" space that surrounds and pervades a mosque is meant to suggest Allah's omnipresence in the world. Architecture, then, plays a key role in focusing the worshiper's attention on God.

Non-Western religious communities also use architecture and the visual arts to facilitate worship, and certain South Asian and East Asian images of the divine are becoming increasingly well known in the United States. As in the West, iconic (or representational) images portray deities in ways that communicate the character of individual gods. For example, certain images of Shiva show him dancing, reflecting the belief that Shiva danced the universe into existence and that he will dance at its destruction. Some images of deities are understood to be more than just representations; if images have been consecrated, then they are traditionally understood to manifest the deity's presence. When the devotee approaches the consecrated image, or *murti*, she enters Shiva's presence and experiences him directly. This is distinctly different from anything we find in the major Western religious traditions, in which representations of the divine are explicitly distinguished from God himself.

Aniconic (or nonrepresentational) images of the gods also facilitate worship in certain devotional practices. The *linga*, often called a phallic symbol, represents Shiva in Hindu devotional practice.[12] The consecrated *linga* is understood to be as full and complete a manifestation of Shiva as any representational image. Aniconic images are not limited to Hinduism; they are found in other communities as well. Tibetan Buddhist *mandalas* (elaborate geometric forms) are often used to represent the universe or even the self, and they often facilitate meditation. Elaborate sand paintings are used in many southwestern Native American tribes. In the Navajo community, for example, sand paintings represent holy beings identified with the life forces that run throughout all living things. In these communities—as in many others—aniconic art facilitates worship just as effectively as iconic elements, bringing the devotee into direct contact with the supernatural.

Scholars face particular challenges when they study visual art that was originally used in the context of worship. For example, many tourists travel to Paris to see Notre Dame, admiring its craftsmanship. For many, Notre Dame is a tourist attraction with great historical importance. Notre Dame's primary purpose, however, was to be a gathering place for worship, an architectural masterpiece that drew the individual's attention to God, the master craftsman. The problem is compounded when religious artifacts—ritual masks or prayer wheels, for example—are displayed in museum collections or traveling exhibitions, completely out of their intended ritual contexts. Crispin Sartwell notes:

> We take an African mask, for example, and encase it in glass in a museum, then we try to appreciate it exactly as we try to appreciate Western paintings . . . But what is missing is precisely the cultural context in which this mask operates: a celebration that includes music, dance, architecture, body decoration, and so forth, and has a very specific religious function. On the other hand, if we *refuse* to bring African masks into our art institutions, because to do so is to falsify them by yanking them out of context, then we may simply be denying ourselves the chance to feel their aesthetic, and for that matter, festive and religious, power. Either way, our experience is impoverished.[13]

The scholar's task is difficult. As we examine pieces that were meant to facilitate worship, we need to take into account their intended ritual or devotional setting.

Music, drama, dance, paintings, and architecture have strong roots in religious traditions. The arts have contributed to individual and corporate worship experiences in all of the world's religious communities because they have great power to inspire religious feeling and to guide devotional practice. The arts, however, have not always been used to encourage commitment to established religious traditions. In fact, one hallmark of the modern period has been the increasing distance between traditional religious communities and modern art. We turn now to the role that the arts have played as a vehicle for challenging religion.

The Arts and Challenges to Religion

Perhaps it was inevitable that the media used for religious education and devotional expression would also become the media used
to level challenges at religious institutions and assumptions. Challenges arose in several forms. First, individual artists used their craft
to challenge institutionally acceptable positions. For example, in the
novel *The Power and the Glory*, author Graham Greene suggests that a
drunken priest can perform God's work better than institutionally
approved representatives.[14] The Vatican condemned Greene's book
because of the questions he raised regarding the nature of a saint.
One cardinal commented: "Indeed novels which purport to be the
vehicle for Catholic doctrine frequently contain passages which by
their unrestrained portrayal of immoral conduct prove a source of
temptation to many of their readers."[15] Institutional disapproval of
individual pieces of art is not unusual. Artists working in many
media have used their art to question mainstream views, either implicitly or explicitly.

The arts challenged mainstream religion in a variety of ways. Most
obviously, artists began to present subjects that institutional authorities found problematic. Paintings, drama, literature, and music available to general audiences began to include works that crossed the
bounds of religious acceptability. Mainstream and publicly funded
art in the modern period began to include subjects that were unacceptable by religious standards. For example, paintings became increasingly sexually explicit. Others, such as the widely popular Harry
Potter children's books, have been condemned for presenting spiritually dangerous beings—witches, wizards—in a sympathetic light.
In addition, some pieces encouraged a secular—rather than religious—orientation to life. Andy Warhol's famous *Can of Campbell's
Soup* (1964), for example, suggested that modern Westerners had
become more intrigued with the consumer goods on their shelves
than with religion. Religious imagery had been replaced by commercial imagery: consumerism had replaced religion in American life.

Finally, artists began to play with and transform well-known traditional religious art and symbols in order to challenge traditionally
held religious ideas. Rather than generating new images, artists
tapped into the emotional power of existing images, and used this
power to make radical, critical public statements. One classic example is Edwina Sandys's *Christa*, a female nude on a cross, clearly functioning as a female Christ figure. *Christa* attempts to expand a tradi-

tional symbol to include women by allowing them to identify with a
female savior. By doing so it suggests that the historical Christian
church has not portrayed women as equal partners with men in the
community. Sandys's piece caused an uproar when it was installed
in the Cathedral of Saint John the Divine (1984) because she replaced the historically familiar male Jesus with an unfamiliar female
Christ figure. For many, Sandys set aside a historical fact (Jesus'
maleness) in order to present a personal, political message.

Religious communities have not been passive in the face of art
that they find dangerous or controversial. When Martin Scorcese
produced his film version of *The Last Temptation of Christ* (1988),
hundreds of Christian groups picketed theaters. The Roman Catholic community publicly opposed a 1999 Brooklyn Museum show exhibiting an image of the Virgin Mary that included elephant dung.[16]
Strong public reactions from religious communities reflect a general concern that the arts have the potential to spread inappropriate
ideas and images in society. Many religious adherents argue that the
arts should point to religious truth or, at least, should generally edify
people. Current debates regarding National Endowment for the
Arts funding arise from questions about the role the arts should play
in the moral life of American society. One of the challenges facing
the arts in the twenty-first century is the relationship between publicly funded art and an increasingly religiously pluralistic society.

The Arts and the Study of Religion

So far we have been examining the arts primarily from the perspective of those familiar with particular religious communities. Devotees use the arts as a vehicle for religious education, expression,
and challenge. Works created for these purposes are oriented
toward an audience familiar with—if not a part of—a distinct religious community. For example, the *Piéta* (1498–99) was crafted to
speak to a Christian viewer familiar with Jesus, the Virgin Mary, and
the Crucifixion. Such art functions within a single religious community, for those familiar with the community's beliefs and practices,
even when it challenges those beliefs or practices. But art can also
provide an entré for students of religion, "outsiders" coming to the
study of a specific religious tradition for the first time.

In the West the academic study of religion still tends to focus on
authoritative textual traditions. Students of Christianity are gener-

ally introduced to the Bible, the writings of the church fathers, and the historical development of orthodox doctrinal positions. Such an approach emphasizes the doctrinal dimension of Christianity—specifically the historically dominant doctrinal dimension—but religious communities are far more complex than this. Numerous scholars have commented on the importance of examining the full spectrum of religious lives and communities. The late Ninian Smart, for example, argues that a complete scholarly study of any community must recognize its mythic, philosophic, ritualistic, experiential, ethical, social, and material dimensions.[17] An investigation of Christianity through the arts could include, for example, the quilts of the Amish, the southern folk art of Howard Finster, or the liturgical dance of contemporary nondenominational congregations. Even mainstream Christian traditions are presented in a more full-bodied fashion when scholars examine the aesthetic elements of religious life, such as Bach cantatas and children's Sunday school art projects.

Artistic elements can also help offset power inequities within religious communities. Authorized texts predominantly introduce students to the religious views of the educated religious elite. Artistic works, on the other hand, often reflect the views and experiences of minority voices. The study of Christianity, for example, benefits from the examination of gospel music, devotional writings of female saints, and evangelical street drama. Authoritative texts present one stream of religious life and thought, but dance, drama, the visual arts, and music can highlight alternative streams of religious traditions.

Religion and the Arts in the Twenty-First Century

As we begin the twenty-first century two factors will become increasingly important in the relationships between religion and the arts. The first is technology. Technological advances have affected the arts since the first clay pot was fired. Twentieth-century technological developments—in film, photography, and the Internet, for example—have provided new media for artists to use. More importantly, modern technology makes it possible to expose wide audiences to music, images, and literature. As a result, ideas and images can be introduced cross-culturally in a matter of minutes. For example, photography and film have popularized religious art and architecture from around the globe, including the *ghats* on the Ganges

River, the Dome of the Rock in Jerusalem, and the Statue of the Reclining Buddha in Bangkok, Thailand. Technological advances will continue to make classic images and stories increasingly available in a public forum.

The second factor affecting religion and the arts is pluralism. The predominance of Christian images in the West is ending. Symbols of the world's major religions—the star of David, the yin-yang symbol, and the crescent—are far more familiar to Americans now than they were just fifty years ago. Pop artist Madonna has almost single-handedly made American teenagers vaguely familiar with Hindu *mantras* and Jewish kabbalistic thought through her music and videos. Elements from every major world religion have crept into the modern West's cultural vocabulary, expanding artistic possibilities as well as creating bridges for communication across religious communities.

In societies such as the United States many artists feel comfortable combining elements from different religious traditions without regard for historical, theological, or cultural differences between traditions. A pluralistic environment provides opportunities for artists to juxtapose images and stories from multiple traditions, transposing elements from one religiocultural setting into another. This is significant because religious communities no longer have a proprietary hold on their own artistic "vocabulary." Ideas and images from one religious community are increasingly related to ideas and images from other religious communities, as well as to society at large.

Finally, pluralism involves the juxtaposition of religious and secular culture, and this raises questions about the nature and purpose of the arts. Giles Gunn has noted that, for some, "literature offers a kind of golden alternative to our 'gong-tormented' world of brass which can provide a religious stay against the confusion of values and commitments which otherwise determine our experience."[18] Many religious communities want the arts to provide a kind of moral bulwark against secular values, and they oppose works of art that neglect or contradict religious values. (Recall that the Taliban in Afghanistan demolished the ancient Buddhist sculptures in the region, arguing that they were "un-Islamic, representing an infidel religion.")[19] This view assumes that the arts always serve religion— and in the modern world this is no longer the case. The arts now have a heritage and tradition all their own, despite a historical connection to religion in the past. Religious language and imagery is used to express universal human sentiments. Artistic streams of influence have developed, with their own vocabulary and history, quite apart from any connections they have to religious life. The Bible, for example, has come to be seen as a significant piece of literature that influenced other great masterpieces such as Handel's *Messiah* and Melville's *Moby Dick*. University curricula reflect this fact, often requiring "The Bible as Literature" for English majors. Art history courses examine painting and sculpture in terms of their contribution to the development of art, not the development of religion. Gothic architecture and various images of the Madonna are discussed in terms of their influence on other works of art, not because they may engender Christian devotion. The growth of pluralism will only amplify the distinction between religious practice and the development of the arts.

Conclusion

This essay began by talking about a young Jewish artist and his use of a cross in a painting of his mother. Asher Lev's struggles reflect his multiple identities as a Jewish man, a painter in the Western tradition, and a member of a modern society. He struggles because he inhabits multiple communities, and the image of a crucifixion generates different responses within these communities. For the Jews in his community the cross is associated with centuries of discrimination and persecution, not to mention a theological heresy. The cross represents pain, oppression, and danger to modern Jews. Lev—quite accurately—anticipates a strong visceral reaction to the incorporation of a Christian symbol in his artwork. At the same time, Lev is a painter trained within the Western tradition. Within Western art the Crucifixion has come to communicate the deepest suffering and anguish of an individual—not just the suffering of Jesus or even of Christians, but of all human beings. For Lev, there simply is no other image within the vocabulary of Western art that will convey his mother's suffering to a wide audience. Late in the novel he thinks that: "There is nothing in the Jewish tradition that could have served me as an aesthetic mold for such a painting."[20] The vocabulary of his home community is inadequate to express the feelings he wants to communicate, so he turns to the vocabulary of a different community. This is not a turn to Christianity, but rather a dip into the secular vocabulary of Western art.

As an artist working in the Western tradition, Lev's choice to use the cross makes sense.[21] But for his audience, this choice poses a challenge. The juxtaposition of a Jewish woman's personal grief and Jesus' Crucifixion requires setting aside the Christianity of the Crucifixion (the religious tradition) and accepting its artistry (the Western artistic tradition). Lev is willing to make this move, but his audience may not be. For them to understand and accept his art they must be willing not simply to increase their visual vocabulary but to learn an entirely new visual language.

Lev's story is fictional, but it reflects the real experience of many artists, including those of the author, Chaim Potok. Potok himself received rabbinical training and struggled with becoming a novelist because of the challenges the art world presented to his upbringing. Potok's identification with Lev is reflected in the fact that he actually painted the controversial painting he describes in *My Name Is Asher Lev*. Acquaintances of Potok's have described their surprise at entering his home and seeing the crucifixion painting "in the flesh," so to speak, hanging on his wall. Potok's struggle reflects the struggle many artists experience. They shift from seeing images as elements of specific religious communities to seeing them as elements of a pluralist artistic community. This shift, in some cases, forces artists—and those who appreciate their art—to reject one community in order to embrace another.

As we begin the twenty-first century, art will increasingly pose this challenge to modern Western audiences. There is less and less consensus about the nature of art, the nature of religion, and the nature of the relationship between these two manifestations of culture. Those of us who feel passionately about art and religion will be forced to think about basic questions: What is art? What makes a work of art religious? Should art fulfill certain explicitly religious functions? Is art "religious" when it raises broad questions about reality without direct reference to a specific religious tradition? Ultimately we will have to answer these questions individually, and our answers will reflect the ways we view the arts in relationship to our individual and corporate identities in today's dynamic and pluralistic world.

Notes

1. The author wishes to thank Gretchen Schoch and Michael Stevens for comments on earlier drafts of this paper.
2. Chaim Potok, *My Name Is Asher Lev* (New York: Knopf, 1972), 329. In the

novel Asher Lev creates two paintings, "Brooklyn Crucifixion I" and "Brooklyn Crucifixion II"; the quoted passage refers to the second painting.

3. Ibid., 330.

4. Throughout this essay I will focus on arts in the West, particularly the United States, recognizing, however, that in recent years Eastern religious traditions as well as new religious movements have gained increasing influence in American society.

5. J. J. Johnson, prerecorded interview, NPR "Morning Edition," 6 February 2001.

6. In Eastern traditions the situation can be somewhat different. For example, traditional Chinese and Japanese theories of art emphasize that works of art reveal the character of the artist. Indian aesthetics also assume an intimate relationship between the artist and his materials. In these traditions the artist may be more properly characterized as a "shaper" or "molder" of material than as a "creator." Throughout this essay I will consider works of art as independent entities, distinct from the artists who created them.

7. Matthias Grunewald, "Isenheim Altarpiece" (ca. 1510–1515), Musée Unterlinden: Colmer. The altarpiece was originally in the chapel of a hospital dedicated to treating diseases.

8. Eliot Deutsch, *Essays on the Nature of Art* (Albany: State University of New York Press, 1996), 82.

9. Eastern religious traditions also incorporated storytelling in a significant way as well. Dramas such as the Japanese Noh plays, which modern Westerners tend to encounter in theater or film presentations, were often originally part of religious worship. The Noh plays, for example, were born out of the melding of Buddhism and Shintoism in Japan in the fourteenth century. They depict the lives of gods, ghosts, and monks, and their performances are sometimes even characterized as offerings to the gods.

10. On a comparative note, Michael Molloy comments: "Although the carpet is not usually recognized as religious art, it is to Islam what stained-glass windows are to Christianity. Both are objects of contemplation for people at prayer . . . A major difference between the stained-glass window and the prayer carpet is that the latter does not depict human images. Instead of portraying figures of saintly persons, prayer carpets often contain a symbolic image of the garden of paradise. At the center of the carpet might be a stylized fountain that sends water in straight lines to each of the four directions and then around the entire border, the four sides of the border representing the walls of the garden." *Experiencing the World's Religions: Tradition, Challenge, and Change* (Mountain View, Calif.: Mayfield, 1999), 441.

11. My companion on a recent airline flight described this Purim celebration in her local congregation.

12. The *linga* is frequently called a phallic symbol, but this characterization misrepresents this aniconic representation of Shiva. The *linga* is more accurately understood as a manifestation of Shiva's cosmic creative energy than as sexual potency.

13. Crispin Sartwell, *The Art of Living: Aesthetics of the Ordinary in World Spiritual Traditions* (Albany: State University of New York Press, 1995), 5.

14. Graham Greene, *The Power and the Glory* (1940; reprint New York: Penguin Books, 1990).

15. Pastoral letter from Cardinal Griffin for Advent 1953. Quoted in Norman

Sherry, *The Life of Graham Greene. Volume 2: 1939–1955* (New York: Viking, 1994), 43.

16. Interestingly, a viewer cannot tell that Chris Ofili's *Madonna* incorporates elephant dung simply by looking at the piece; we only know because he told us.

17. Ninian Smart, *Dimensions of the Sacred: An Anatomy of the World's Beliefs* (Berkeley: University of California Press, 1996).

18. Giles Gunn, *Literature and Religion* (New York: Harper & Row, 1971), 4.

19. Ian Chai, "Taliban Threatens Buddhas," 27 April 1997, <http://chip.cs.uiuc.edu/~chai/berita/970401–970501/0078.html>.

20. Potok, *Asher Lev*, 324.

21. Potok's fictitious painter is not the only Jewish artist to use a crucifixion. Elie Wiesel describes a child's execution drawing on crucifixion imagery. See Elie Wiesel, *Night*, trans. Stella Rodway (New York: Bantam Books, 1960). More obviously, Marc Chagall's *White Crucifixion* (1938) incorporates a crucifixion as the central, dominant image.

How to Read a Church

Peter W. Williams
Miami University

AFTER houses and retail stores, one of the most abundant and ubiquitous features of the built landscape of the United States is its churches—or, more broadly, houses of worship. From giant metropolises like New York and Los Angeles to tiny crossroads hamlets such as McGonigle, Ohio, one or more church buildings are virtually essential to bestowing ontological status on a place; without a suitable site for public worship, a gathering of buildings is simply that—a nameless cluster—rather than something that can be experienced as a community. Like houses and stores, though—and perhaps even more so—not all churches are alike. They differ considerably in such particulars as size, shape, style, siting, age, ornament, interior arrangements and furnishings, and the materials from which they are constructed. In both their general patterns of construction and distribution as well as in their individuality churches can be interpreted as markers of a community's social, cultural, and historic identity. To understand their significance, one must learn to *read* them—to see them not just as generic icons of religiosity but rather as particular embodiments of that cultural impulse, simultaneously unique and representative. This essay is an attempt to provide the beginnings of a vocabulary and grammar for such a task of reading—primarily of Christian churches, which dominate the American landscape, but also of Jewish, Islamic, Hindu, and Buddhist houses of worship which increasingly compete for visual attention in a nation in continual demographic transformation.

At the most basic level, churches (a term I shall use generically to mean "buildings for worship") are physical constructions; whatever their metaphysical implications, they are necessarily built—literally from the ground up—out of components such as brick, stone, wood, glass, concrete, and the like. The catalogue of components that make up a church is inconclusive in itself but can provide some preliminary clues as to the building's character and context. Wood, for example, is usually cheaper than stone, unless the latter is unusually plentiful (and/or the latter scarce) in a particular region. In many circumstances, then, a wooden church is a sign that the congregation that erected it is of modest size and means. The local abundance of a particular material may also lead to some interesting regional stylistic variations; where the Gothic style in Europe was usually executed in stone, in parts of the United States brick or wood may be a substitute. Such adaptation is usually more a matter of necessity or opportunity than intention, but the results—such as the "carpenter Gothic" style popularized by the Anglican architect Richard Upjohn during the mid-nineteenth century—can be dramatically innovative and aesthetically pleasing. It may also come to constitute a regional style that transcends denomination, visually linking together churches ranging from Eastern Orthodox and Episcopalian to Methodist and Baptist. (This frequently happened in the American West during the later nineteenth century.) In more developed and prosperous urban situations, congregations may rise above such exigencies and build grander churches of stone, even when that material has to be imported at considerable cost.

Scale and *siting* are two other related physical characteristics of a religious building that need to be factored into any informed "reading" of a church. "Scale" is more or less synonymous with "size," although it implies that size has to be gauged in relationship to other structures in the vicinity or to similar structures elsewhere. Together, these factors have considerable impact on how a church is experienced by those in visual contact with it. A diminutive parish church sandwiched between larger buildings in the midst of an urban residential or commercial block, for example, sends a different message about its status and role in its community than does a giant cathedral sited in lonely splendor on a hilltop. The message here may be as much one of intention as of means: Roman Catholic churches erected during the late nineteenth and early twentieth centuries, especially in cities, were often deliberately overbuilt—designed on a much larger scale than their constituencies required—in order to make a political statement about the actual and hoped-for role of the church in the community. Denominational rivalry and status anxiety have sometimes egged religious groups on in trying to establish a more imposing local presence than that of their counterparts.

Another motive for, or result of, building on a grand scale is the possibility of programming in ways that smaller or even medium-sized congregations could not afford or sustain. Another important material clue here is not just the size and character of the worship space itself, but that of the entire *plant* which accompanies that space. Only the very smallest churches usually provide only space for worship. Most also provide office space for clergy and support staff; an assembly hall for congregational functions, such as community meals and meetings, often accompanied by a kitchen; educational facilities, ranging from one or two classrooms to entire wings or buildings filled with such spaces; nurseries and other places for day care for children too young to attend regular worship or instruction; auditoriums for lectures or dramatic productions; and, in the largest sorts of complexes, gymnasiums, bowling alleys, and other large-scale recreational facilities. Apart from the main plant may be auxiliary structures such as housing for clergy (variously known as the *rectory, parsonage,* or *manse*); elementary schools (favored by Catholics, Missouri Synod Lutherans and, in more recent years, various evangelical groups); housing for their personnel (e.g., convents for teaching sisters assigned to staff Catholic parish schools); burial grounds, especially in the country; parklike areas with grottoes or religious statuary; and, more mundanely, parking lots. In this latter connection, siting can also be logistically significant; many larger recently built evangelical churches are located near the exit ramps of interstate highways, in the hope (frequently fulfilled) of drawing a constituency not simply from a local "parish" area but from an entire metropolitan complex. (Fleets of school buses have yielded to vast parking areas as evangelicals have risen on the socioeconomic scale.)

Even signage can be revealing. More traditional churches generally have a prominent but discrete signboard in front giving the church's name, denomination, times for worship, and possibly the names of the clergy. Many evangelical churches use more conspicuous signs—sometimes movable—which, in addition to basic information, display a Bible verse or clever saying with a religious message. Active evangelism and disdain for the norms of middle-class taste both seem to be at work here. The names of churches are also significant. Roman Catholic churches are generally named after saints or some aspect of the divinity, e.g., "Holy Trinity." Episcopal churches follow a similar practice, though usually confining their repertoire of saints to biblical figures and those associated with the British Isles, e.g., Saint George. Mainline Protestant church names usually avoid suggestions of the holy and are more geographically descriptive, e.g., "Oxford Methodist Church." Numerical designations, usually "First" or "Second" (occasionally down to "Fourth" or more, as in Chicago's "Fourth Presbyterian"), are often employed by denominations in the Reformed tradition, such as Presbyterians, Congregationalists (United Church of Christ), and Baptists, to indicate the order in which that church was founded in a particular community. Lutherans have their own usages, often favoring names such as "Zion," "Faith," or "Christ." Evangelicals often avoid the designation "church," preferring terms such as "tabernacle," "temple," or, more recently, "Christian Life Center," on the theory that only the congregation itself is the "church."

The size and character of a parish plant can tell us a great deal about the nature of the community that has built and now supports it. ("Parish" is used here specifically to refer to the entire membership and physical apparatus of a local religious community rather than simply a building for worship.) At one extreme, Christian Scientists have traditionally built only an auditorium for public readings and testimonials, with few additional facilities to sustain a broader communal life. At the other extreme, many of the Southern Baptist, Pentecostal, and other evangelical "megachurches" built during the last few decades include extensive facilities for educational and recreational activities. Some, such as the prototypical Willow Creek Community Church in South Barrington, Illinois, which resembles a shopping mall more than a traditional house of worship in its overall contours, even includes a food court. The "institutional churches" of mainline Protestantism—for example, Chicago's Fourth Presbyterian or Cleveland's Pilgrim Congregational—built in many cities during the late nineteenth and early twentieth centuries were the predecessors of today's megachurches; though their scale was not quite as grand, their strategies of drawing in congregants through elaborate programming, often as much recreational as formally religious, anticipated in many ways those of their latter-day evangelical counterparts. The elaborate K–12 educational programming of pre-Vatican II Catholicism was aimed not so much at bringing in newcomers through evangelistic outreach as it was designed to keep those already in the faith, especially recent immigrants, from succumbing to the allures of Protestant religion and/or secular society. On the other hand, the relatively modest efforts at mounting programs beyond worship and the correspondingly modest plant size of contemporary "mainline" Protestant churches indicate a high level of comfort with the surrounding social order, although the sometimes dramatic attrition in membership experienced by those denominations—American Baptist, Disciples of Christ, Episcopal, ELCA Lutheran, Presbyterian (PCUSA), United Methodist, and United Church of Christ—in recent decades may have resulted in part from that very sense of being "at ease in Zion."

Considerations of siting may include relative positioning within a community—on downtown street corners, in residential neighborhoods, at interstate exits, and so forth—as well as the kinds of communities in which denominations choose to locate. Catholics and Eastern Orthodox, for example, not surprisingly tended to build churches in urban working-class neighborhoods during the period of the New Immigration (ca. 1870–1917), while Methodists had earlier erected their own often modest frame structures in every rural small town and crossroads that the traffic would bear. Church location, also not surprisingly, has tended to follow demographic shifts; many once-grand downtown Protestant churches have since World War II either closed down, adapted to new ethnic constituencies, or sold their plants to Asian, African American or Hispanic newcomers as their traditional patrons abandoned the cities for the suburbs. (Roman Catholics have done the same, often consolidating two or three parishes in response to population change as well as an acute clergy shortage.) Concomitantly, the suburbs, which now contain a majority of the nation's population, have seen extensive new religious building since World War II, first among Catholics, mainline Protestants, and Reform and Conservative Jews and, more recently, among evangelicals of every stripe. Although some older urban churches remain prosperous, others have been abandoned, razed, "recycled" by newer groups, or converted to secular uses. (One former Catholic church in Pittsburgh is now a brew pub.)

Along with scale and siting, *architectural style* is a significant component of a religious building's identity. Although in recent years some local religious communities, such as the previously cited Willow Creek Community Church, have deliberately tried to shed an identifiably religious visual identity, most American religious groups have consciously designed their buildings in a manner evocative of a specifically religious tradition. In colonial North America, this often involved an adaptation—usually a down-scaling and vernacularization—of styles then in fashion among coreligionists in the mother country. Anglican churches along the eastern seaboard during the eighteenth century, for example, reflected the Wren-Gibbs neoclassicism that had been so successful in London following the Great Fire of 1666 which had wiped out much of that city's medieval building. Before long, Puritan Congregationalists, Baptists, and other dissenting groups were in turn adapting the styles that had been introduced by what they had perceived as an oppressive, worldly, and heretical elite. During the nineteenth century, religious groups of all sorts, from Jews to Catholics to Methodists to Swedenborgians, joined in the national enthusiasm for one stylistic revival after another, beginning with the Roman and yielding successively to the Greek, the Romanesque, and the Gothic (with even the Egyptian making occasional inroads). For Roman Catholics and Episcopalians, the medieval revivals made a certain amount of sense, since these communities had historical lineages and liturgical practices consonant with these styles. For Baptists and Methodists, though, neither of these continuities could be plausibly argued; the appeal was instead to fashion, to solidarity with the iconographical expression of the identity of the broader community, or in some cases to shifting notions of the meaning and character of worship.

During the twentieth century, style in religious buildings has gone in two different directions. Southern Baptists, at one end of the spectrum, have deliberately opted for a "retro" style—usually colonial revival—which is symbolic of patriotism, rootedness in the American landscape, and "traditional family values." Other conservative groups, such as the Willow Creek Community Church cited earlier, continue the old auditorium style as well, but housed in an outer shell that might be mistaken for a shopping mall, conference hotel, or suburban office park. Some wealthier and more sophisticated congregations have turned to "signature" architects, such as Frank Lloyd Wright or Louis Kahn, to design structures in a "Modern" or "Post-Modern" style, with little reference to the traditional symbolism of Christianity and a reliance on the play of shapes, material, and light for setting a religious tone. Most post-World War II Catholic and mainline Protestant churches, for which worship patterns have converged, have developed a standard suburban profile, blending tradition and the techniques of Modernism to accommodate the post-Vatican II emphasis on interactive worship (new for Catholics) and a more elaborately ritualized liturgy (new for Protestants) in structures that either adapt the traditional rectangular church shape or introduce a semicircular groundplan.

In addition to exterior style, the interior apparatus of a church plant can be very revealing of a congregation's character. The most elaborate plan is characteristic of traditional Catholic, Episcopal, and some other churches whose worship involves an elaborate, formal liturgy. Such churches are generally rectangular in shape, reflecting a hierarchical arrangement of the space inside, and, where American circumstances permit, literally *oriented*, with the altar facing east, the direction in which the sun rises and which, according to tradition, Jesus would return again. In this plan, which is not often used for newer churches, the building for worship is formally divided into several areas, each with a similarly formal, Latinate name.

Narthex. The narthex is the space one enters when one steps through the main entryway, and is fundamentally a vestibule or transitional area between outdoors and indoors. Here can be found coatracks; pamphlets stands; candles to light for special intentions; containers for holy water, into which worshipers may dip their fingers as an act of ritual purification upon entering; and other features which are preparatory for worship. This is a space in which greeters may be positioned to welcome newcomers and worshipers mill about and converse quietly before worship begins.

Nave. The nave is in the worship area proper and is usually entered through a set of doors separating it from the narthex. (The name comes from the Latin *navis*, or ship, which the interior of a church may resemble in inverted form, or which might be a metaphor for an interconnected community.) This is the space in which worshipers sit during the worship service itself and usually is outfitted with horizontal rows of *slip pews*. (Some colonial-era churches still have *box pews*, designed to accommodate a family, which are rectangular and have hinged doors on one side. Other alternatives are *cathedral seating*—movable banks of attached chairs—or, in some old-style Eastern Orthodox churches, no seats at all.) The seating in the nave is usually divided by a central aisle, which is used by the congregation for access and by those leading the worship—clergy, assistants, choir—for processionals.

Sanctuary and *choir.* The sanctuary (from Latin *sanctus*, "holy") stands at the far end of the nave and is usually separated from the rest of the worship space by a set of steps. The altar itself, on which the communion service is conducted, may further be separated by a low railing. (Some Anglo-Catholic churches emphasize this separation by a medieval-style altar screen between the nave and choir, while Eastern Orthodox churches have a set of "royal doors" through which the priest disappears for the most solemn part of the consecration.) Only the celebrant and his or her assistants (*acolytes*) are usually permitted in the sanctuary. Some churches also designate an area between the nave and sanctuary, the *choir*, to accommodate the singers—descended from medieval monastic choirs, the members of which sat facing one another in front of the sanctuary. Cushions for kneeling in front of the altar or in the pews may feature embroidered designs with Christian motifs.

Chapel. The term "chapel" denotes a place for worship smaller than a church. This may take the form of a niche to the side of the main altar, in which a smaller altar dedicated to a particular saint, such as the Virgin Mary, may be placed; to an additional worship space outside the main church set aside for private devotions or small services; or to a place for worship in an institution such as a prison, boarding school, college, hospital, asylum, or airport. (In Britain, the term is used by dissenting groups wishing to distinguish their places of worship from those of the Church of England.)

Roman Catholic, Anglo-Catholic Episcopalian, and Eastern Orthodox churches may also utilize a variety of other aids to the sacramental worship which characterizes their traditions. The latter tradition is notable for its use of *icons*, that is, stylized two-dimensional paintings of Jesus, the Virgin Mary, and the saints, which are placed in a specified order around the walls and in the dome of the church as well as on the altar screen, or *iconostasion.* The other Catholic traditions utilize paintings and or sculpture in the sanctuary, as well as the *Stations of the Cross*, a set of fourteen paintings or sculptures on the themes of the narrative of the Passion of Jesus, arranged in order along the walls of the church and used for Lenten devotion.

In addition, all of these traditions employ what Anglicans call "liturgical stations": physical aids to conducting necessary parts of worship. These include the *baptismal font,* which ranges in scale from a simple basin to an elaborate marble or carved wooden structure with a wooden cover of Gothic design. (This may be located in the *gathering,* or expanded narthex, of a modern Catholic church; immediately inside the entrance to the nave; or adjoining the sanctuary.) Next to it may stand a *paschal candle,* lit for the vigil of Easter. Other stations are a *reading desk* or *lectern,* from which scripture is read; a *pulpit,* from which the sermon, or interpretation and application of the Word, is delivered; and the already mentioned *altar,* traditionally a block of marble, on which the *elements* (bread and wine) of the eucharistic service are consecrated. (More recently, many churches utilize instead a movable wooden table.) An array of implements of ceramics, metal, or other materials may also be employed in the preparation and distribution of the Eucharist, such as a *chalice,* or cup with a base, for the communion wine. *Hosts* (pieces of communion bread or wafers) which have been consecrated but not consumed during a eucharistic service may be kept in a receptacle known as a *tabernacle* (Roman Catholic) or *aumbry* (Anglican), usually accompanied by a lit candle or bulb. A *cross* or *crucifix* and candles (*torches*) mounted on wooden poles may be carried in processions. During the service, the priest and other participants wear *vestments*—ceremonial garments derived from ancient Roman usage, with corresponding Latinate names—together with similarly color-coded (for the liturgical season) *paraments* (or *frontals*) which are hung over the altar, pulpit, and desk. Special garments and hangings used during the service are stored in an adjoining room known as the *vestry* or *sacristy.* (Eastern Orthodox use Greek terms for many similar items.) Lutherans and, more recently, other mainline churches such as Methodists and Presbyterians, utilize some of the same material apparatus for worship, though usually in less elaborate form.

The arrangement and contents of a church such as that described generically above are geared to an ideal of worship based on the regular celebration of the *sacraments,* that is, rituals originating in the ministry of Jesus and the Apostles and intended to mediate divine grace, or saving power, in material form through ritual action. Roman Catholics and Eastern Orthodox count seven sacraments, although they differ slightly in this enumeration. Anglicans and Lutherans, following Protestant custom, restrict these to two—Baptism and Eucharist—as the only ones specifically instituted by Jesus, although Anglicans designate the other five rituals recognized by Roman Catholics as "sacramental actions." Whatever the differences, the underlying concept behind this sort of worship is the notion that material objects and gestures, together with verbal formulas, are the basis through which humans encounter the divine. As a result, the physical setting for worship is taken very seriously, and employs both spatial arrangements and material accompaniments that are designated by a precise vocabulary as well as strict directions for implementation. (The amount of beeswax in altar candles and the specifics for the cloth draped over the altar are variously stipulated by Roman Catholic and Anglican manuals.)

At the other end of the liturgical spectrum, churches in the Baptist, Holiness, and Pentecostal traditions usually are devoid of this elaborate array of spatial divisions and liturgical implements. The emphasis in these services is usually on the preached Word, vocal music with instrumental accompaniment, and, frequently, testimonials by members of the congregation. Although such worship generally follows traditionally prescribed if only implicitly acknowledged patterns, emphasis is often put on spontaneity rather than formality. Congregational seating may take the traditional form of slip pews but often is modeled on that of theaters, beginning with the "auditorium church" of late nineteenth-century American cities in which fixed, adjoining, folding, cushioned seats ("opera seating") were arranged in curved tiers, providing a good view of the stage for the entire assemblage. Opposite the seating was a raised platform, or stage, with a dominant pulpit front and center. In front of the pulpit would be a table for the administration of communion (with the wine often in small individual glasses arranged in a circular tray with suitable openings to be passed among the congregation). Behind the pulpit might be seating for the choir, with a large pipe organ providing a backdrop. In Baptist churches, the platform might also contain a concealed tank (*baptistry*) in which baptism of adult believers by complete immersion could be practiced at appropriate times.

Although Presbyterians, Congregationalists, and Methodists often built in this form in its heyday a century or so ago, these denominations have largely abandoned the auditorium church for one more suited to a formal liturgy. Evangelical groups today still utilize it in modified form, with an array of instruments and amplification devices often replacing the pipe organ of old. The Victorian decor, such as heavy wooden pulpits and stained-glass windows, may be gone, but the essential form of the auditorium church still persists, with the traditional Protestant focus on the spoken and sung word. Evident also is the *aniconic* tradition of Reformed Protestantism, which, from the time of its founders Calvin and Zwingli, adopted the Old Testament prohibition on "graven images" and thus banished virtually all forms of visual arts from the place of worship. During the past century or so, this prohibition has been modified to some degree through the introduction of pious portraits of Jesus, such as the once-ubiquitous rendering by Warner Sallman.

One way of understanding the contrast in these physical settings for worship is through the typology of *church* versus *meeting house*. Another way of making the same distinction is through the Latin phrases *domus dei*—"house of God"—and *domus ecclesiae*, or "house of the congregation." The first model fits the elaborate house of worship described first above, and suggests that the building utilized for worship is in some way a sacred place itself and has to be treated with proper respect. Ceremonies of consecration (and, occasionally, deconsecration, when a church is turned over for secular use) utilized by Roman Catholics and others emphasize that such structures have a special character that sets them aside from "secular" structures, such as houses, stores, and offices. (Houses may in fact be blessed and contain special places for the display of religious objects, but cannot ordinarily be utilized for formal public worship.) On the other hand, reformers such as Calvin and Zwingli in Reformation-era Switzerland rejected this model for worship entirely, and declared that any appropriate setting could be utilized for Word-centered Christian worship—an attitude adopted by the Puritan movement in Elizabethan England and shortly thereafter translated to New England as well. Puritans in the latter colonies devised a new kind of structure they called the *meeting house* for their own notion of worship, which was the forerunner in essentials of similar places used by many evangelicals today. The meeting house was explicitly not a place where divinity resided but rather a setting in which a congregation of believers gathered to hear the Word preached. The same space could be, and was, used by townspeople for "secular" functions such as education, government, and even defense against Indians.

Although this distinction in places for worship held fairly true along Catholic/Protestant lines through the nineteenth century, and is still reflected in many churches remaining from that era, it is now true primarily at the extremes of the spectrum: Anglo-Catholic and Eastern Orthodox at one end, and Southern Baptists and Pentecostals at the other. Roman Catholics, Episcopalians, and many mainline Protestants have converged in their approaches to worship and corresponding notions of proper space for worship in recent decades, and the contrast between their churches built since World War II is consequently much diminished. Typologies for thinking about "sacred space" and for categorizing types of religious space should thus be utilized with care, since many places for worship do not fall cleanly into one or the other of these pairs of opposites.

We have already seen that religious buildings are primarily designed to provide space for worship suitable to the liturgical needs of particular traditions, even though the boundaries of some of these traditions may have begun to blur in recent decades. We have also seen that many churches provide not only worship space but also facilities for a potentially wide variety of activities that constitute a congregation's programming. In addition, there are still other identities and activities associated with religious buildings and their constituents that need to be discussed in order to provide a fuller sense of possibilities of "how to read a church."

Especially in areas of early European settlement—for example, the Atlantic seaboard and the Southwest—churches may possess the identity of historic buildings, and may be included on the National Register of Historic Places. (Whether religious buildings should be subject to preservation ordinances designed to protect the character of historic sites is currently the subject of considerable legislative and judicial controversy.) The historic character of a particular building might have to do with its being the oldest representative of a particular tradition in a given area; its association with historic events and personalities within a denominational tradition; or, in the case of the Old South Meetinghouse in Boston, its having served as the site of important "secular" activities, in this case the events leading up to the American Revolution. (Many colonial churches, such as New England meetinghouses and Spanish missions, served civic as well as religious functions and still often help constitute civic landscapes.) Churches may call attention to their historic status by displaying plaques, offering tours, and even maintaining gift shops where the visitor may purchase coffee mugs, tote bags, note cards, and the like with suitable illustrations. Tours conducted by parish volunteers should often be taken with a grain of salt, since such guides frequently stress what is oldest, largest, and most expensive to the detriment of more insightful historic interpretation.

A church may also be notable for its architecture and/or art. Some architects of note specialized in ecclesiastical design—Ralph Adams Cram, Patrick Keeley, Richard Upjohn, and Henry Vaughan, all practitioners in different versions of the Gothic revival mode—and their work is notable both as aesthetically accomplished and as influential in promoting particular styles as normative for subsequent religious building. In the latter category one might add the handful of churches by H. H. Richardson, such as Trinity Episcopal in Boston, which, though few in number, nevertheless established the "Richardsonian Romanesque" as a distinctive American Victorian style for civil as well as religious building. Other "signature" architects such as Frank Lloyd Wright and Philip Johnson have designed religious buildings, but their attention and influence have generally been elsewhere. On the other hand, many structures designed not by professional architects but rather by local builders, such as those that bedecked countless New England town greens beginning in the eighteenth century, have survived as masterpieces of excellent design as well as historic and civic icons.

Churches are sometimes repositories of religious art as well. Roman Catholics have led the way here, since their tradition has always valued the material expression of religious themes for liturgical and devotional usage. As soon as American Catholics became wealthy enough to afford religious art and architecture (such as that of Patrick Keeley, mentioned above, who designed hundreds of Catholic churches during the later nineteenth century), their churches frequently overflowed with paintings, sculpture, wood carving, and other ornamentation. Some of this was imported from France and not of high aesthetic quality; others, such as innumerable stained-glass windows crafted in Munich, remain treasured. The 1950s saw a flurry of indigenous design with the liturgical renewal movement that helped inspire the worship reforms of Vatican II; the latter ecumenical council's dictates led to the renovation of the interiors of many American Catholic churches and cathedrals to adapt them to a more participatory mode of worship, with mixed aesthetic results.

Within the (loosely designated) Protestant traditions, Anglicans led the way in the North American colonies through the introduction of architectural design based on the modes of London—often creatively adapted to colonial circumstances—and also in the introduction of liturgical art in the form of communion silver sets, many of which were donated by Queen Anne and still on display, especially in Virginia. Stained glass did not become common until after the Civil War, when work by Tiffany Studios and John LaFarge, among others, created an opalescent glass style of great beauty. (This glass was sometimes introduced into the windows of older churches, with a striking, not to say incongruous, stylistic contrast as the result.) During the early twentieth century, Connick Studios of Boston revived the very different mode utilized in medieval cathedrals, which suited well the architectural design of contemporary medieval revivalists such as Ralph Adams Cram. Cram and other revival architects also took advantage of the availability of European craftsmen and set them to work creating fine pieces in metal, wood, and other media. Where Catholics and Episcopalians generally stayed close to medieval tradition, some Protestants ventured farther afield in their attempts to depict contemporary religious heroes—in the case of the First Baptist Church in Washington, D.C., an image of "Mister Average Baptist" in stained glass.

Cathedrals, which began to proliferate among Catholics and Episcopalians in the rapidly growing cities of the post-Civil War era, have emerged as particularly prominent examples of the coming together of sacred art. Catholic cathedrals generally tend to commission art specifically for their own use. Episcopalians have in some cases—such as Saint John the Divine in Manhattan and Grace on San Francisco's Nob Hill—utilized cathedrals as veritable art museums, incorporating into their liturgical decorative schemes a wide variety of both contemporary and historic art works, often the result of munificent wealthy donors. The stained glass in these cathedrals may also combine the traditional panoply of saints with newer themes, such as images of Albert Einstein and John Glenn in the glass at Grace and a piece of moon rock in a specially designed window at Washington's National Cathedral.

Just as churches may serve as art galleries, so also do they sometimes serve as concert halls. Much colonial religious music consisted of unaccompanied congregational singing, especially in New England, where Puritan theology forbade the use of hymns of human composition. (Psalms, presumably of divine inspiration, were the crucial exception.) By the time of the revolution, most religious communities had overcome any early antipathies toward hymn-writing and singing as well as instrumental music, and the pipe organ began to become a common piece of church furnishing. After the Civil War, Protestant urban "auditorium" churches modeled on theaters or concert halls featured vast organs as the backdrop to the pulpit platform, which latter also was often spacious enough to accommodate a sizable choir. Professionals were sometimes employed (and still are) as "ringers" to set the pace and pitch for volunteer singers.

African Americans developed their own tradition of choral music, with the Fisk Jubilee Singers leading the way in adapting the spirituals of slavery to more European musical standards, and Thomas A. Dorsey and others in the twentieth century creating the gospel music now performed by vested choirs in many black churches. White southern evangelical churches developed their own gospel tradition, often performed by male quartets. (Such churches frequently have percussion instruments available on stage together with the usual organ or piano.) The Mormon Tabernacle Choir in

Salt Lake City gathered an ecumenical following in its rendering of Christian standards such as Handel's *Messiah*. Other churches incorporate secular classical pieces into their services as preludes and postludes and open their facilities for chamber music concerts and similar recitals by their own organists or other musical professionals. Since many churches have suitable acoustics, seating, and instruments, especially organs and pianos, their use for the presentation of appropriate (according to their tradition) musical pieces seems reasonable enough.

The National Cathedral in Washington, begun near the turn of the twentieth century and not completed until 1990, also illustrates some other functions which churches and cathedrals may exemplify. The National Cathedral was envisaged as a "house of prayer for all people," a church that transcended denominational identity and which could thus serve as a setting for events, such as sermons by and funerals of prominent figures, that would help create a national religious culture. (Saint John the Divine in New York aims to serve a similar role for the arts and for social causes.) Bishops as well as ministers of prominent individual churches—Jerry Falwell of Thomas Road Baptist Church in Lynchburg, Virginia; Congressman Adam Clayton Powell of Abyssinian Baptist Church in Harlem; Martin Luther King (both senior and junior) of Ebenezer Baptist in Atlanta; and Cardinal John O'Connor of New York's Saint Patrick's Cathedral—have served as prominent spokespersons for their religious communities on public issues, and their cathedrals or churches have become closely identified with them as civic centers. Urban churches, beginning with the Social Gospel movement in the late nineteenth century, have also frequently sponsored social ministries, providing shelters, soup kitchens, and other means of relief for the homeless, drug addicts, and others in need of assistance. (The narthex of the elegant Saint Bartholomew's Episcopal Church on Manhattan's Park Avenue has at times been lined with cots for those with no other shelter.)

Yet another function of religious buildings is to function as burial sites. In colonial or later rural churches, parishioners were often buried in plots immediately adjoining the church. In some cases, interment has actually taken place within the house of worship itself on the medieval model; the mortal remains of Woodrow Wilson, for example, reside in an aisle of the National Cathedral, and many churches especially in the south have walls bedecked with commemorative plaques sacred to deceased congregational members, even though their actual bodies lie elsewhere. Another approach involves the *columbarium*—from the Latin for "dove cote"—in which the ashes of the deceased repose in small cubicles within the parish plant. In a few cases, such ashes may be collectively buried in a plot next to the church building. In most cases, though, the remains of the deceased in whatever form are buried in cemeteries, whether denominational or nonsectarian, which are often arranged in a park-like atmosphere reflecting new attitudes toward the dead and the natural order generated by early nineteenth-century romanticism.

So far, we have been using the word "churches" ambiguously—to speak of houses of worship generically, but mainly, as the word itself usually suggests, places of Christian worship. Even the latter, as should be clear by now, are by no means homogeneous but run the gamut from *domus dei* to *domus ecclesiae*, from Russian Orthodox to Pentecostal, with quite a number of variations in between. However, even though the population of the United States has always been predominantly Christian, other religious groups with their own distinctive places for worship have gradually augmented the nation's religious landscape. Although there is not space here to discuss every group represented in the nation—nearly all are—it may be worth noting a few of the more distinctive features of those religious traditions that have made a significant mark, from Jews—present in small numbers from the beginning—to Muslims, Buddhists, and Hindus, who have arrived in significant waves primarily since the revision of immigration quotas in 1965.

Jews in the United States (and to a lesser degree elsewhere) have divided themselves into three major denominations, or traditions—Reform, Conservative, and Orthodox—and do not agree on terminology for their places of worship. The two latter, and more traditional, groupings use *synagogue*, a Greek-derived word adopted during the time of Jewish dispersion among the Hellenistic empire and signifying a place of public assembly (though some Orthodox congregants still refer to the actual edifice using the Yiddish designation, *shul*). More liberal Reform Jews, on the other hand, deliberately chose in the nineteenth century the term *temple*, even though their places of worship have little in common with that built by Solomon in ancient Jerusalem. They use the name rather to make the point that the normative condition of Jews is *diaspora*, or dispersion throughout the world, and that the ancient dream of restoring the Jerusalem temple should be abandoned. In American practice, this verbal distinction has not been reflected in architectural expression.

The latter, however, has been problematic since Jews, so long accustomed to living amidst gentile host cultures, have never developed a distinctive architectural style. Rather, beginning with the Touro Synagogue in Newport, Rhode Island, in 1763, American Jewish building has adapted the styles of their Christian neighbors. By the mid-nineteenth era, urban synagogues/temples were often designed in an eclectic combination of Gothic, Romanesque, and Moorish (that is, Mediterranean Islamic) elements. Since World War II, new Jewish construction, overwhelmingly suburban, has employed the techniques of architectural modernism and, in keeping with Jewish *aniconic* tradition, avoids the representation of the deity in material form. In terms of interior design, more traditional Jewish houses of worship, beginning with the Touro Synagogue and continued especially among ultra-Orthodox or Hasidic Jews, segregate women in balconies, sometimes even with porous screens, while men are seated on the ground level. While seating arrangements vary somewhat among Jewish groups, virtually every synagogue or temple has a *bema,* or reading platform; an *Ark of the Covenant,* in which are kept the sacred Torah scrolls when not in liturgical use; and a *Ner Tamid,* or eternal light.

If Christians of all stripes are counted together, Jews have for long been the second largest religious community in the United States. Recently, however, immigration from the Middle East and south Asia has increased the American Muslim population to a number approaching and possibly exceeding that of American Jews. As with other religious newcomers, American Muslims have often adapted to American circumstances by converting any conveniently available space, such as a house or storefront, into use as a *mosque,* or place for worship. As the Muslim community has grown and prospered, however, it has erected mosques specifically designed for the purpose of Islamic worship. On the exterior, such mosques frequently incorporate the traditional elements of design utilized in Muslim countries, such as a dome and minaret, or tower from which the call to prayer is issued five times daily (where local practice permits). The interior of the mosque is an open area where believers may prostrate themselves in prayer. As in Judaism, figural representation is prohibited, but the walls may be decoratively inscribed with geometric designs or verses in Arabic from the Quran. Also as in the most traditional forms of Judaism, space is separated along gender lines, with women often relegated to a basement level. The only other features are likely to be a *minbar,* or pulpit, oriented to Mecca, and a *mihrab* (or *qiblah*), that is, a niche indicating the direction of Mecca, the holy city of Islam, and thus pointing the faithful quite literally in the right direction—a particularly important reminder in a non-Muslim society such as the United States. Facilities for ritual ablution and temporary storage of shoes may be found at the entrance to the worship space. Accompanying the mosque may be an Islamic center—similar to Jewish community centers—which provide educational and recreational facilities for an area's Muslim community. Since in larger metropolitan areas that community is likely to be drawn from a wide variety of Muslim countries, the style of design may represent an accommodation to these distinctly North American cultural circumstances.

The same is true of Hindu temples in the United States, which have in recent years begun to appear in many major metropolitan areas—usually suburbs—but which differ in some important ways from their south Asian prototypes. Typical American temples may include a *gorupa,* or tiered gate, suggestive of the Himalayan mountains, and a *garbha-griha* (literally, "womb-house"), which contains images of a variety of Hindu divinities. A major difference between North American and south Asian temples is that the latter are usually dedicated to a particular deity associated with a particular place; the former, much like Muslim centers, have to accommodate immigrants from all across India, and therefore often feature a wide variety of images. These are usually found along the periphery of an open hall; instead of communal worship, priests are generally engaged by individual families to perform rituals (*pujas*) in front of favored images or else in homes.

Buddhist temples in North America vary considerably, given the wide variety of ethnic groups which practice particular sorts of Buddhism as well as a multitude of native converts usually attracted to Zen or Tibetan varieties. A Zen meditation center will generally have no images but rather feature an open space for the practice of *zazen.* Temples in traditions that emphasize devotion rather than meditation may feature a prominent image of the Buddha on a central altar, which becomes a focus for chanting. Flanking this central figure often are subsidiary images of various "saints" such as arhants and bodhisattvas. Nichiren temples will have an altar featuring a copy of the Lotus Sutra, a particularly sacred text for them, while Tibetan temples may have prayer wheels as an aid to meditation. The interior of some older Pure Land temples may resemble a Christian church, with pews, an organ, and hymnals, although the image of Buddha Amitabha and murals of the Pure Land, though similarly placed, differ markedly in content from those that might be found in a Christian church. Also prominent in Japanese Pure Land temples are images of the denominational founders, such as saints Honen and Shinran. Exteriors may reflect a variety of national styles, including a pagoda-shaped or egg-shaped (*stupa*) elevation on the roof.

Still further discussion could be given to other recent religious imports, such as Jainism and Sikhism, or to the distinctive iconography of Latino Catholic churches; the variety of American religious design, like American religions themselves, is endless. We might end with a few more generic thoughts about the levels of interpretation that might profitably be brought to bear on any particular example of religious architecture.

Material. All religious buildings are made of specific materials and sited in particular settings. This material level of composition is the most basic and tells us significant things of an economic and geographical sort.

Functional. Religious buildings are erected as appropriate shelters for particular forms or ritual activity as well as related educational, charitable, and other works mandated by particular traditions. Reading the interior layout of a building and inventorying the liturgical apparatus that accompanies it can give us a good sense of which tradition is being served and what its physical needs may be.

Stylistic. All buildings beyond shacks and hovels possess some sort of design, however rudimentary, which is seldom entirely original. The sources of a particular building's design may include particular national and ethnic as well as religious traditions and may also reveal linkages to either "high style" or vernacular building modes in the "secular" realm.

Symbolic. A religious building may symbolize a number of things, from the relationship of its worshipers to what they regard as the sacred to their relationship with the broader social and political community in which they are situated. Religious symbolism may be overt, as in the use of stained-glass images or crosses atop a steeple, or indirect, as in the absence of such overt symbols.

Religious buildings, like other sorts, are complex and condensed sources of meaning and need to be consciously interpreted, using a variety of tools derived from liturgical theology as well as from social and architectural history. That act of interpretation may in turn reveal a great deal about a particular house of worship and its builders and users, possibly more than they ever consciously intended.[1]

Notes

The author wishes to acknowledge valuable suggestions from Grant Barber, Aaron Hughes, Jeanne Kilde, Alan Miller, and Liz Wilson.

1. For further reading the author's bibliographical essay on American religious building compiled for the *Material History of American Project Newsletter* is available on the web. See "The Built Environment of American Religion: The State of the Art," at www.materialreligion.org/journal/archbiblio.html. In the area of styles and elements, Paul and Tessa Clowney's *Exploring Churches* is British-oriented but provides a useful guide to style, ornament, and implement as well as a brief history of Christian religious building (Grand Rapids, Mich.: Eerdmans, 1982). Marcus Whiffen's, *American Architecture Since 1780* is useful in identifying the major styles of American building, including churches and synagogues (Cambridge, Mass.: MIT Press, 1992). A more extensive discussion of architectural styles in American historical context is Alan Gowans's *Styles and Types of North American Architecture: A Cultural History* (New York: Icon, 1992). Sarah Hall's *The Color of Light* is a good introduction to stained glass (Chicago: Archdiocese of Chicago Liturgy Training Publications, 1999).

There are two general surveys of American architecture and religion. The author's *Houses of God: Region, Religion and Architecture in the United States* surveys the development of American religious building from a regionalist geographical perspective, stressing the impact of ethnicity (Champaign: University of Illinois Press, 1997). Marilyn J. Chiat's *America's Religious Architecture* discusses representative buildings in every state (New York: Wiley, 1997). Both contain extensive bibliographies. In addition, a few significant studies have been produced recently that are not cited in the bibliographical essay. See Karla Goldman, *Beyond the Synagogue Gallery: Finding a Place for Women in American Judaism* (Cambridge: Harvard University Press, 2000); Paul Eli Ivey, *Prayers in Stone: Christian Science Architecture in the United States, 1894–1930* (Champaign: University of Illinois Press, 1999); David Kaufman, *Shul with a Pool: The "Synagogue-Center" in American Jewish History* (Hanover, N.H.: University Press of New England, 1999); Jeanne Halgren Kilde, *Church Becomes Theatre: The Transformation of Evangelical Architecture and Worship in Nineteenth-Century America* (New York: Oxford University Press, 2001).

Textures of a Religious Life:
The Vernacular Religious Art of
Sister Ann Ameen

Leonard Norman Primiano

Cabrini College

As the days went by I longed to do something for Jesus in the mission field. One afternoon, I was looking out the window watching a young man building a house. He had it all sheeted up with black Donna Kona [tar siding]. As I looked, a man's hand appeared. It moved across the [surface]; and as it moved, a beautiful picture began to take shape. There was sky, sea gulls, a duck pond, trees, flowers, and an old fashioned cottage. The sunset was crimson. Oh, what colours, what beauty. I heard myself saying, "Why that is hooked." The hand held a rug needle like grandmother used to use on her rag mats but this looked like yarn. I kept looking at this beautiful picture until it faded away as if it had never been. The soft voice spoke. "Child, you can do that." But I would need a frame, mat needle and burlap yarn to do it. The soft voice again spoke, "I will provide." I walked away from the window wondering how these things would be.

But they keep stable the fabric of the world, and their prayer is in the practice of their trade.

The workings of the mind and the touch of the hand live eternally in artifacts.[1]

THIS essay introduces to the public a significant vernacular religious artist, Sister Ann Ameen (1908–1998, fig. 1).[2] Little known outside her home region of Newfoundland, Canada, she combined a sensitivity to her community's traditions of art and craft with her own unique vision of the divine.[3] As a long-time resident of both Newfoundland and the United States, Ameen is a uniquely North American religious artist who negotiated her knowledge and

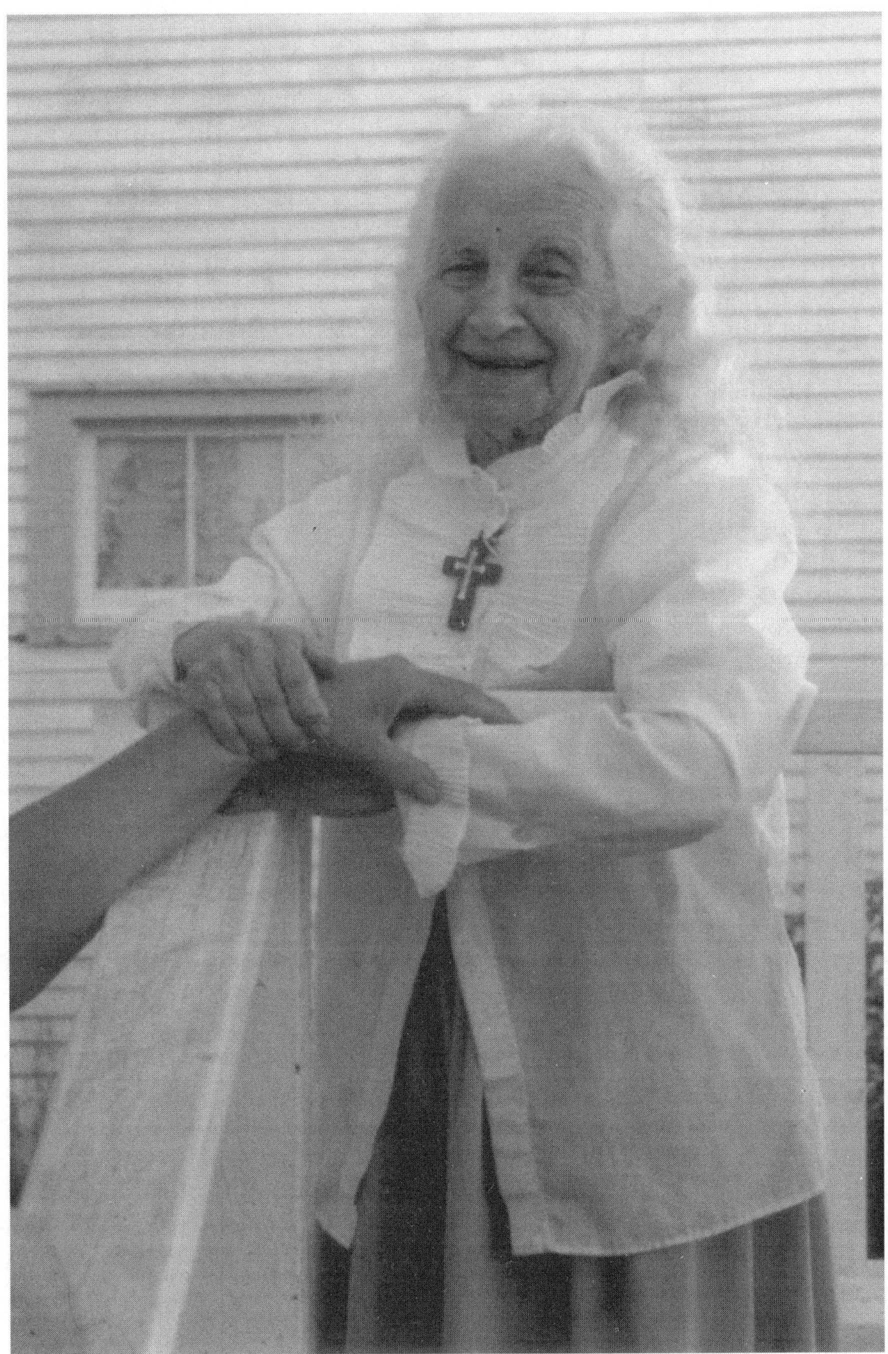

Figure 1. Sister Ann Ameen, August 1996. Photo, Leonard Norman Primiano.

experience of both Canadian and American Christianity. Ameen's unique "picture rugs" and "scripture rugs" embody her understanding that these mundane objects can function as didactic religious art, expressing her own Christian beliefs while working to transform the beliefs of those who behold them. I had the opportunity to know Sister Ann Ameen personally during the last five years of her life. In the summer of 1995, she even allowed me to live in her home for several days and photograph many of her hooked "mats."[4]

Sister Ann Ameen was a petite (4′10″ tall) missionary who died in 1998 at the age of ninety. She described herself in the second of three self-published spiritual autobiographies as "the little woman who lived very plainly so that souls across the sea could learn of Jesus."[5] Married multiple times, Annie Francis Sharpe Hansen Ameen Brown called herself "Sister" not because she was a Roman Catholic woman religious, but because she was a sister in the Lord Jesus Christ dedicated to spreading the message of evangelical Christianity to anyone who would hear it.

Sister Ann Ameen was born in 1908 in the rural community of Shearstown, Conception Bay, in the eastern part of Newfoundland.[6] Her father, Martin Sharpe, was a sea captain and an Anglican. Her mother, Elizabeth Snow, was a Methodist. There was a singular and insular homogeneity to Newfoundland's primarily English and Irish population at this time. In many ways, this insularity exists into the twenty-first century. The restrictions of living in an isolated "outport" disturbed this spirited and attractive teenager. The occasion for Annie Sharpe's escape came in the form of an advertisement from a Rhode Island dentist for a mail-order bride. His positive response to her letter presented the opportunity to leave Newfoundland, and so began Sister Ann's noteworthy and colorful activities in the United States. This departure was only the first of many for Sister Ann. After a short time, she also exited from this first marriage due to, in Sister Ann's words, "sexual incompatibility" with her older spouse. Moving down the east coast, she was hired and had success as a ballet dancer and chorus girl in the New York burlesque circuit. This career was cut short because of a toe injury, as well as a scandal; Sister Ann, posing as British royalty, had an adulterous affair with a married member of New York society. When the man's wife sued Annie Hansen to cease and desist, her deception was uncovered, and after a suicide attempt, she was taken to Bellevue Hospital for psychological evaluation. These details were reported in the 7 December 1928 edition of the local Newfoundland newspaper, *Bay Rob-*

erts Guardian, no doubt to the utter embarrassment of her family in that close-knit community.[7]

It was after these tumultuous incidents that she had a conversion experience and began, in her own words, "fifty-five years knowing Jesus." Accompanying her through at least ten of those years was her second husband, The Reverend Kattar Ameen, a Lebanese Christian she met in Florida. They both attended a Church of the Nazarene Bible School in New York state, and proceeded to establish an evangelical ministry in Danbury, Connecticut, along with a home for the elderly. She returned to Newfoundland in 1958 after the death of her husband, closing the American chapter of her life. There, she began a forty-year private and public odyssey of moving from house to house, promising to complete buildings, self-promoting her various projects for charitable contributions, and creating a Christian cottage industry by hooking mats to gain financial support for everything from mission activities in Asia and Africa, to her Newfoundland "homes for wayward girls," to her small Bible study classes. She actually traveled in 1982, her seventy-fourth year, to Bangladesh for five months to visit the people to whom she had consistently sent contributions and many King James-version Bibles.

During one of my extensive interviews with her from 1994–1997, I asked: "What is your theology—are you a pre-millennial or a post-millennial Christian?" She responded, "I'm sure Jesus didn't use those words." I again inquired: "And Sister Ann, are you a folk artist, a Canadian artist, a Newfoundland artist, or a religious artist?" "A Christian artist," she replied, "that's how I would describe myself."

Trained in the early decades of the twentieth century, first in the Church of England in Newfoundland, and then in the Methodist and Holiness traditions of the American denomination known as the Church of the Nazarene, she was a painter who occasionally used oil-based and acrylic paints but who most frequently used wool and acrylic yarn to communicate a message of fidelity to and love of God through the art of hooking rugs. These "paintings in wool," as she called them, were inspired by her religious and cultural background and the actual voice of her God consistently telling, commanding, prompting, urging her to express her Christian beliefs.

Ann Ameen's religious beliefs can be placed within the very broad category of Protestant Evangelical Christianity. Such a term designates those churches, like the Church of the Nazarene, that emphasize the teachings and authority of the Scriptures, especially of the

New Testament, in opposition to the institutional authority of the Church itself, and that stress as paramount the tenet that salvation is achieved by personal conversion to faith through the atonement (that is, through the life, suffering, and death) of Christ. As a corollary to this faith, believers are required to spread the gospel as a part of their expression of belief in God. It, however, is inaccurate to limit Sister Ann to any particular denominational affiliation. Her lived religion, like her hooked rugs, illustrates a belief system influenced by and interpreted through her many contacts with religion in North America.

It is vital to remember when documenting and analyzing the material expression of religious belief in general that it is not sufficient merely to study a static religious object among many objects but to attempt to understand a context of meaning and the use of religious artifacts for artists and their communities.[8] The verbal, behavioral, and material expressions of belief are a part of community and individual religious culture, whether found in formal or informal art forms. By the material expression of religious belief, I mean artifacts, interior and exterior environments or landscapes, and architecture that are individual and communal expressions of religious belief, affiliation, or faithfulness. Such religious material culture can be further delineated using sacred, decorative (or aesthetic), and functional categories. Like any material culture, the material expression of religious belief can be specifically observed in paintings, drawings, prints, sculpture, photography, books, foodways, clothing, bodily alterations and adornment, architecture, agriculture, town planning, furniture, furnishings, and even machines and devices. Religious material culture can include everything from a statue of Saint Joseph in a contemporary Catholic kitchen placed in a location of honor because of a promise made to the saint,[9] to the festive foodways of holiday occasions, and from the aesthetic of plainness in a colonial Puritan or Quaker home, to the colorful hooked rugs emblazoned with religious images and words for display in home or church.

Strong influences of community and self have concerned scholars who study the visual production of artists such as Sister Ann, and they have fashioned terms to classify such artists and their work as "primitive," "naive," "self-taught," "folk," "outsider," "visionary," "idiosyncratic," "found," "grassroots," "isolate" "intuitive," and "art brut."[10] Folklorist Terry Zug offers a solid scholarly description of the folk artist as acquiring "knowledge and skills through a longstanding, informally transmitted, regional tradition." The work of the "outsider artist," for Zug, could draw on past experiences, but the "artistic impulse comes from deep within and is intensely personal in form, execution, and meaning."[11]

The deficiency of all such concepts is that they do not leave sufficient room for understanding the nuanced relationship between individual creativity and community influence. In the case of Sister Ann, she is not adequately described by either of these categories of folk or outsider artist. Her rugs are both regionally traditional and deeply personal. Her output as a religious artist emerged from a craft tradition transmitted to her by family and community. Ameen created her rugs to sell to a community which would immediately recognize and understand the form she was using. Her work, however, is completely individualistic, even idiosyncratic, in her treatment of the hooked rug as a religious object, in her use of color, and in the subject matter of her creations.

What, in the end, is so distinctive about Sister Ann's "paintings in wool"? Ameen's art is the material expression of her vernacular religion, religion as she interpreted, negotiated, and created it. She took the traditional Newfoundland craft, the hooked mat or rug, and transformed it into a religious object. One of the standards of the hooked and sewn rug genre has been that "religious themes, although common in other household handicrafts, are hardly ever found in hooked rugs. As these rugs were made to be walked on, religious subjects were probably considered inappropriate."[12] Ann Ameen's rugs, her vernacular religious art, are the exception to this rule. By her own estimation, Sister Ann Ameen hooked over twelve hundred mats, everything from small mats in the traditional "welcome" size ($20'' \times 34''$), to medium size ($28'' \times 56''$), to what can be called her "monumental" mats (the largest of which, "The Rapture," measures $79'' \times 142''$). For a woman only four feet ten inches tall, hooking this particular rug when she was over eighty years old, such production was a remarkable physical as well as artistic accomplishment.

Residents of St. John's recall seeing her in the window of her various shops in the city in the 1970s and 1980s hooking hour after hour, day after day. She developed a technique which allowed for swift rug production. Such speed could account for her enormous output.[13] To create the pile surface, Sister Ann usually used not torn rags but acrylic yarn (which she called wool) positioned below the stretched burlap. The hooking tool (a bent nail driven into a wooden handle with a "vee" notch filed into the edge of the rod at the tip) was inserted between two strands of the weave, engaged the yarn, and brought it above the surface of the burlap where a loop was made.[14] She repeated the process in the same spot making a second loop, then she moved along several spaces in the weave and repeated the steps.

Sister Ann's linear process of hooking allowed for an impressive visual impact, but her "lower loop density"[15] did not allow for a durable product. Her textiles are not thick and heavy like typical hooked rag rugs. They could not be put in a washing machine to clean them. If soiled, they have to be washed by hand in cold water like a wool sweater. One, of course, could be disappointed with the feel of these objects but never with their appearance. Still, there was a reason for Sister Ann's technique. It was because these textiles were made not to be placed on the floor but on the wall. Such treatment was Sister Ann's response to the tradition that you would not want people to walk on religious rugs. Her art had a pedagogical as well as a mnemonic purpose. Sister Ann believed that all her rugs were religious rugs, although some had no overt message or orientation (either people requested them or they simply sold well to tourists): "I was praying while I was hooking [it], that's what makes it religious."

Unlike other Newfoundland artists (for example, Gerald Squires)[16] who incorporate the stark beauty of the province's grey, dark, cold, harsh yet beautiful vistas, Sister Ann's view of the Newfoundland landscape in wool and acrylic is of her own invention. Her colors are vibrant, even effervescent, like the public face of her personality and her effusive belief in the glory of God and the wonder of creation. "I loves [*sic*] bright, cheerful colors," Sister Ann noted, "whites, light pinks, light blues." Sister Ann also hooked her vision of the landscape where Jesus lived. In countless instances, she created a terrain combining both places: Newfoundland as Holy Land and Israel as a country of Atlantic fishing outports. This vision meant the presence of both palm trees and lighthouses, of sea birds on the coast and angels around the tomb.

Canadian art writer, Peter Gard, has described Sister Ann's use of color as "outrageous." He has written that "they are as bright as a kid's toy and as subtle about faith as a Jehovah's Witness at the door."[17] When I wanted to understand her use of color and why her mats were so bright, she pointed me to the wild flowers and weeds growing outside her front door. "Look at their color," she explained, "they are bright like all of God's creation." Her hooked rugs or mats in some way attempt to mimic the radiant colors of creation including the sun and, naturally, could never be dour or dull. In her personal diary, Sister Ann specifically addressed the colors of nature and how God presented them to humanity:

What a wonderful Heavenly Father we have to give us the Beauty of His Colours. Summer the Beautiful flowers. Autumn. The crimson and gold on His trees. Winter the snow in all its glistening white, and the spring with its soft green grass and Lilac trees . . . yes we have a very great and very Holy God and I wonder how many of us looks [sic] up toward Heaven in the run of a day and whispers thank you Dear God.

In the final years of her life, Ann Ameen lived in Bay Roberts, a community about an hour out of St. John's, in buildings she called her Beacon Light Bible School and Bethany House. This complex consisted of the remnants of a restaurant, store, and a central two-story structure by the bay in which she occupied the only heated room. She hoped that the structure named "Bethany House" would be the location of a "home for wayward girls" that she had spoken about for thirty years but which never came to fruition. For the most part, she lived alone in Newfoundland after her return to the province from the United States in 1959. She said that she accepted a life of loneliness and solitude as a part of her duty as a missionary of Jesus' message, and this motif of waiting alone for someone to come and for something great to happen is also found in her art.

A reading of Sister Ann's three-volume collection of writings, which mentions in some detail her activities with Reverend Ameen, could lead one to assume that her return to Newfoundland occurred as she mourned the death of her beloved husband. I confidently thought that her mats first created in the years after her return were, in the words of Barbara Kirshenblatt-Gimblett, "objects of memory"[18] of her beloved spouse and their many years of devoted marriage and work together. Her dead husband, however, never appears in her mats. When I asked to see a picture of him, she could not or would not provide me with one. There were no images of him in her living quarters. She told me, during my stay with her in 1995, that their marriage, in fact, dissolved in the United States when her husband fell in love with another woman, Ruth, a nurse who worked in one of the couple's nursing homes in Connecticut. Sister Ann returned to Shearstown, her birthplace, to escape the bad memories of her husband's infidelity, his divorce of her in Mexico, and finally his unfortunate death along with Ruth in a Florida automobile accident.

Her creations still remain memory objects, though, if not of her husband, of her life as a child waiting for her seaman father to return, of the stern discipline and religious nurturing of her Methodist mother, and of the special attraction that Newfoundland itself holds for natives as a place they long for after they leave it. This intrinsic connection to the wind-swept island is the reason why Newfoundlanders become teary-eyed when they sing their former national anthem, "The Ode to Newfoundland." "The weather is beautiful [here]," Sister Ann told me, "if you like fog, rain, and wind . . . Our Newfoundland is a good tyrant." It, therefore, is possible to see in Sister Ann's mats correlatives of memory,[19] that is, images from everyday life which correspond to another person or thing in the past: a lighthouse, a church, a ship, Scripture passages, and other subjects which are central to her life. Of course, the challenge is trying to figure out what images fit what memories and experiences and when and if these things actually happened to her.

Sister Ann acknowledged that a reason she lived such a solitary life was because people shied away from her constant attempt to engage them in conversation about religion. Partly self-serving, partly evangelical strategy, she would press visitors to talk about their religious lives simply to allow herself an opportunity to give her own life history. She did this conversing with strangers, individually or in a group setting, through an outpouring of continuous narratives, many of them exquisite memorates, personal tales of supernatural encounters about how God constantly touched her life. She spoke of how Jesus, in the form of a little boy, visited her in her garden when she was a young girl, about her own healing from cancer through a vision, about how God provided her with bags of money when she needed it for a project, even about how God told her not to eat the inside of bananas. In addition to her rugs, these narratives represented a significant display of her religiosity. Their enactment, in fact, was in obedience to what she perceived to be the voice of God. Therefore, when she gave her testimonials to visitors, she employed two voices: her own and the voice of God, her "heavenly Father." Her performances of these personal religious narratives were the oral explications of her material paintings in wool, and her hooked mats were the materialization of her individual religious beliefs. The irony of the way she turned local inhabitants away from her in the last ten years of her life was that she desired a consistent audience to whom to relate her stories. For this reason, she especially enjoyed first-time visitors, because such occasions would allow her the opportunity to conjure the miraculous story of her life again. The opportunity to tell such spiritual narratives anew is an important expressive mode for elderly religious individuals and communities because it allows them to relate both the central beliefs important to their lives and situate themselves within larger religious narratives.[20]

Sister Ann never connected herself to a specific congregation or denomination in Newfoundland, such as the Pentecostal community or the Salvation Army. She deliberately remained outside such affiliations to retain her own independence. She loved the attention that the media could give to her and her Christian message, maintaining a very public profile on local radio broadcasts, in public appearances, and even on television. Still, she enjoyed living on the margins and being a woman of mystery. She shared few private confidences with friends, neighbors, or other Christians. To spend time with Sister Ann was also to witness how she engaged in not just telling her story to others but how she consistently reinterpreted her autobiography to her listeners. Like any competent and sensitive performer, she altered her stories at each telling so that they would have the greatest effect on her listener. This act of consistently editing her life led one artist, who curated a 1995 exhibit on her hooked mats at the Art Gallery of Newfoundland and Labrador, to note that Sister Ann was "the ultimate post-modernist, her life is a novel, and she rewrites, re-presents, and revises it daily."[21]

It is often assumed that a mother passes the techniques of hooking rugs onto her daughter, but Sister Ann indicated that her mother never actually gave her instruction in the technical method for creating a rug. She did, however, grow up in a household where both her grandmother and mother were active rug hookers, and she did observe them in their craft. Ann Ameen did not actually begin hooking her mats until she was in her mid-fifties in Newfoundland, with her greatest production coming as she grew older. What her mother did teach her was that hooked rugs could be aesthetically pleasing and that they were objects to be respected. It was Ameen's understanding that just as these simple objects expressed beauty and commanded respect, they could also convey powerful messages about life and God. As noted in other folkloristic perspectives on elderly men and women, Sister Ann Ameen

proudly [took] credit for her personal discovery of a medium and form
for recasting [her life . . . She] forged distinctly individual solutions to
common needs: in the process . . . [affirming] the creative potential in
the expressive culture of the elderly and the centrality of life review in
this period in the life course.[22]

Steeped in paradox, she credited both God and herself for the creation of the rugs.

The artistic options of Newfoundland women and their hooked
rug traditions suggest both a received style consistently using geometric designs and a personal and innovative style using a diversity
of designs from outside the community's repertoire. In the latter
case, any model could be borrowed, from a pattern in another textile to a scene from a printed source. Folklorist Gerald L. Pocius,
writing on Newfoundland hooked rugs, notes that "even printed
words could serve as a design source . . . The highest degree of innovation with design sources involves the mental assemblage of ordinary objects into an image to be used specifically for a rug, and not
merely an attempt to copy a concrete holistic model."[23] Sister Ann
Ameen rarely produced geometrical designs. Out of forty mats in
her home that I once had the opportunity to examine and photograph, I found only one with geometric designs. Her mats were intended for the wall, not the floor. She learned from her mother that
picture rugs are special—they were not used in the kitchen—and
Newfoundlanders would customarily not step on special rugs. Her
paintings in wool would teach their owners about Christianity and
deserved the same respect that one would give to the Bible or some
other religious object such as a chromolithograph of a religious subject in one's home.[24] Her rugs follow the personal and innovative
pattern because they are religious and, as she would say, "God inspired." Considering her consistent use of religious words and/or
images as well as very bold colors, Sister Ann's creations both follow
a tradition of design innovation within this Newfoundland aesthetic
and represent the highest degree of innovation within that tradition.[25]

One of the noteworthy themes of twentieth-century Christian iconography has been the way radical individuality and political environments have caused artists to integrate local or indigenous forms
into Christian visual culture. The art of African-American Christians
has produced dark-complected figures of Jesus in the United States,
and the "liberation theology" of Latin and South America has been

expressed visually in paintings of scriptural passages using images from everyday life in Nicaraguan base communities.[26] As already noted, Sister Ann's rugs are a significant example of her personal negotiation of local and universal subjects and sites serving as Christian symbols—from blue shore lines with geese to the fires of hell with ominous blackened birds. What is particularly dramatic about them as integrative artifacts of belief is how these objects are a testimony of her journey through North America's religious cultures.

Catherine L. Albanese, in her assessment of the way scholars have formulated consensus histories of American religion, has suggested that the religious identity of Americans bears "the signs of contact with those who were other and different . . . the shape and operation of American religious life—all of it—is best described under the rubric of religious combination."[27] Sister Ann Ameen, daughter of Newfoundland, long-time resident of the United States, is an intriguing bicultural example of North American religious contact, combination, and exchange. The possibility of such exchanges between United States and Canadian religion seems a natural extension of Albanese's thesis applied to the richness and vitality of Sister Ann's art.[28]

Why Sister Ann would seek out such encounters can best be understood within the context of religion in Newfoundland. At the turn of the twentieth century when Ann Ameen was born, religious life on the island was both restrictive and segregated. One lived in distinctive Roman Catholic, Church of England, or Methodist Christian communities.[29] In Conception Bay North, where Sister Ann was raised, settlement patterns marked religious affiliation geographically. Newfoundland remains to this day a land where people can identify the religious affiliation of individuals and where they lived on the island simply by hearing their family name. The separation between the Christian denominations was well understood by inhabitants. Interaction between Roman Catholics and Protestants was strained and marriage between them socially unacceptable. Sister Ann's mother was a Methodist and her father an Anglican, and her home of Shearstown lay in the staunchly Protestant communities of Conception Bay North. It is quite possible that she had little contact with Catholics or even other Protestant groups in her formative years.

Her arrival in the United States was undoubtedly a shock to her religious sensibilities. She experienced there something unique to her: the plurality of American religion. Eventually she would even

marry a Lebanese Christian man, and together they would seek out
evangelical forms of Christianity. Such contact deeply influenced
her visual expression of religion. From the deeply pluralistic American environment she drew an imaginative religious vocabulary that
made space for a variety of Christian iconographic forms.

Representative of the color and energy of American culture and
the traditional elements of Newfoundland craft, it is possible to divide Ameen's designs into three categories. The first is the conventional Newfoundland hooked rug subjects such as a flower, a welcome mat, or a geometric design; as Sister Ann told me, "anyone
can do a flower in a mat." These mats were religious because she
willed them to be so (fig. 2). The second category is her "paintings
in wool," that is, a picture without words or with only a few words—
ideal, ordered, perfectionist landscapes populated by sea birds and
palm trees, lush foliage and explosive sunsets. She felt these rugs
were her most significant creative contribution: "Naturally [these
rugs] are religious . . . looking at it puts you in the mind [of reli-
gion]."[30] Often employing overtly religious motifs such as doves,
churches, and angels, her proportions sometimes distort reality, but
she felt she was offering a realistic rendering. Most importantly, she
painted a "concept" that Jesus Christ was always among us; she tried
to place Christ within the context of people's everyday lives (figs. 3,
4). The third category is what Sister Ann referred to as her "black-
boards." Here she choreographs words and images creating a visual
religious text. These mats impose words over images, integrate
words into images, and surround script with a colorful border or
background accompanied by representational figures (fig. 5).
Ameen's tools for teaching Scripture, they also represent her em-
bodiment of scriptural words as image, her hooked illuminated
manuscript art. These are words or phrases usually from the New
Testament but without the biblical citation. Ameen assumed that the
viewer recognized the biblical source text. Related to this category
are her monumental rugs, which can be six feet tall and sometimes
eight feet across, containing script and/or images, and which took
her up to six months to complete. A continuation of her practice of
transforming Christian words into Christian images, these rugs were
created for sale and display in public settings such as churches,
schools, and even government administration buildings (fig. 6).

This feisty little woman took a traditional understanding of design
and production of hooked rugs and shifted their function to match
a religious meaning and purpose rooted in what was important to

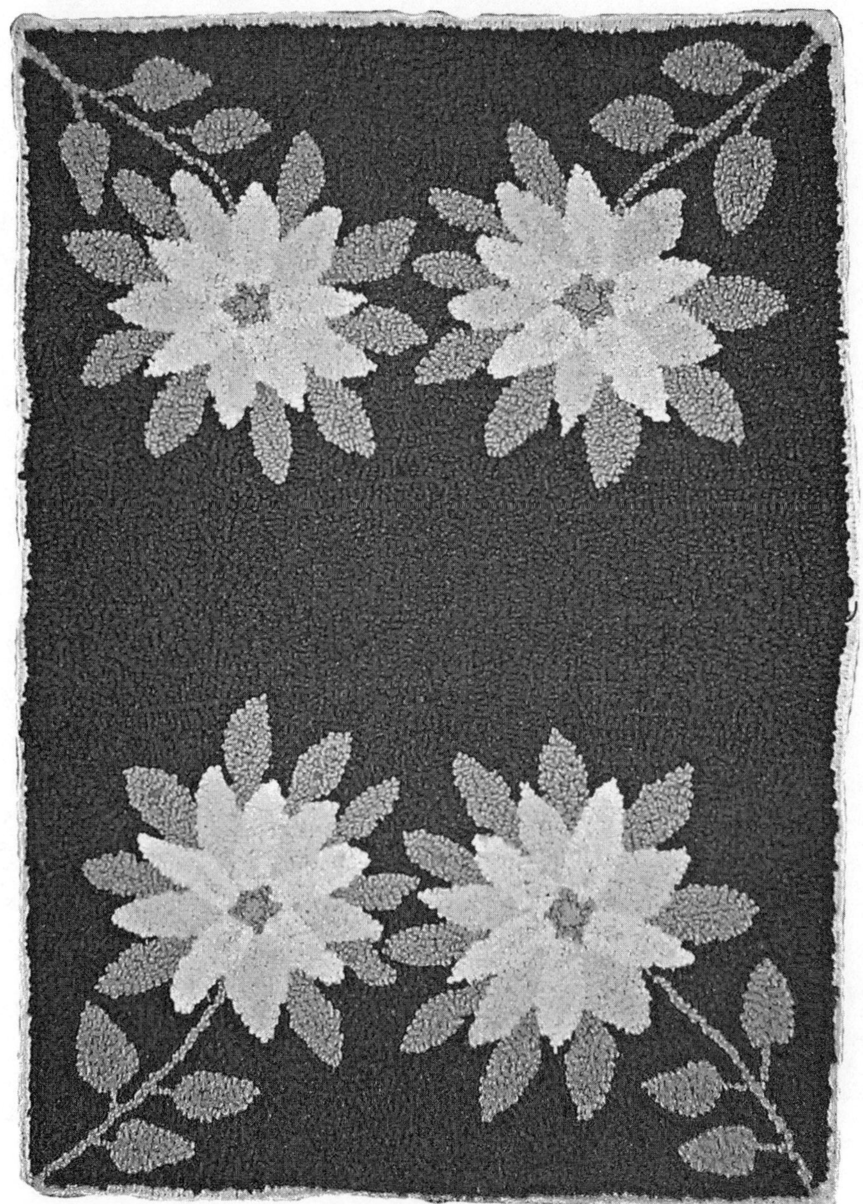

Figure 2. Yellow Flowers on a Purple Background, n.d., 26.5 inches × 38.5 inches. Collection of Leonard Norman Primiano. Photo, Don Dempsey.

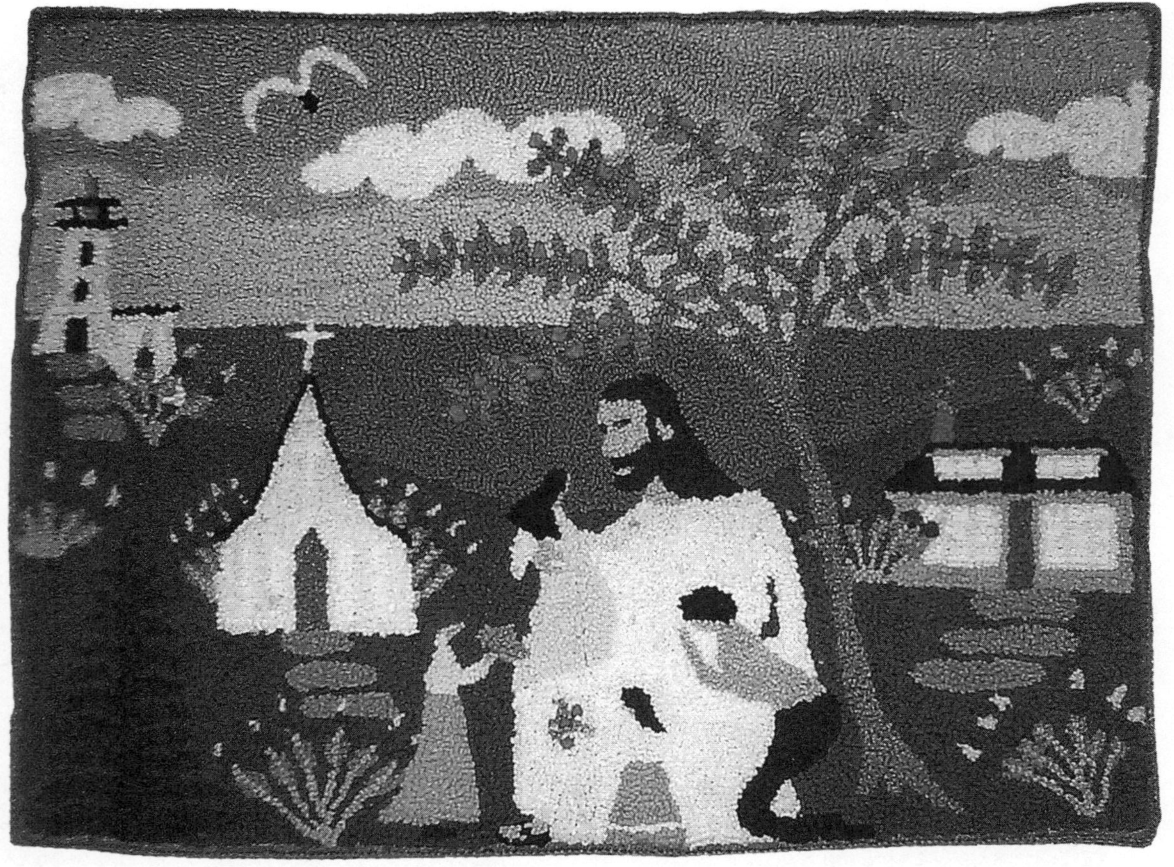

Figure 3. Jesus with the Children, n.d., 26 × 38 inches. Collection of Leonard Norman Primiano. Photo, Don Dempsey.

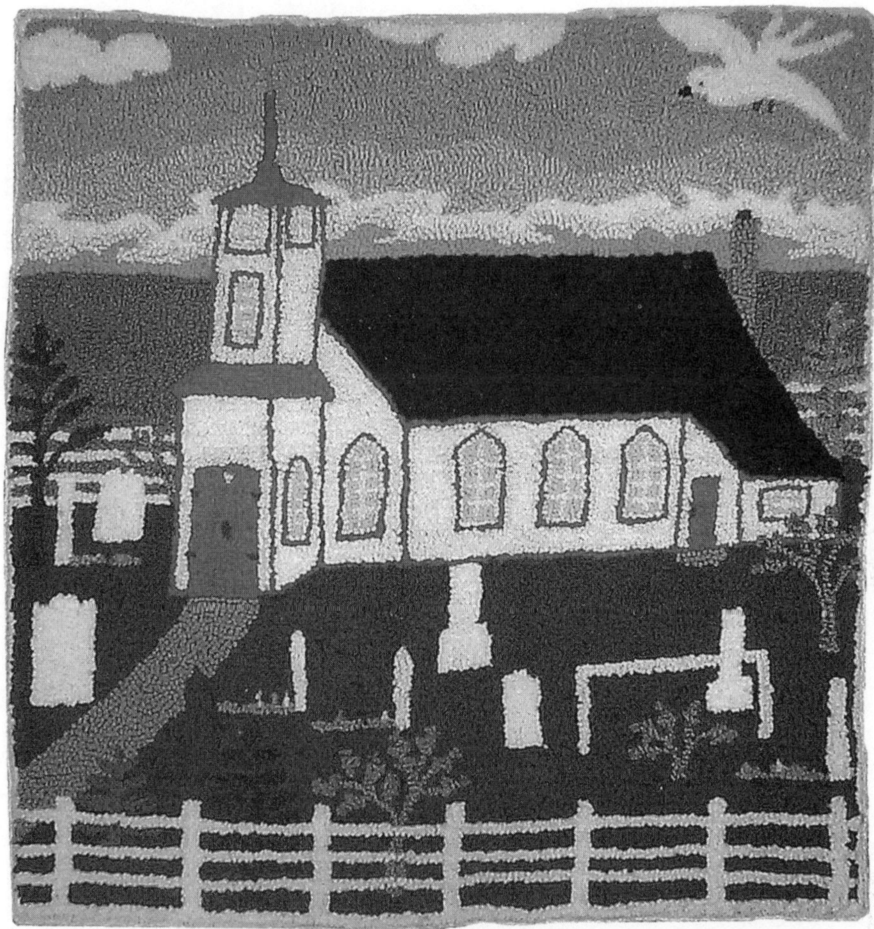

Figure 4. Church with Red Door, n.d., 38 inches × 35 inches. Collection of Leonard Norman Primiano. Photo, Don Dempsey.

her understanding of the religious life. Sister Ann, both insider and outsider, combined her Protestant evangelical sensibility with its emphasis on biblical text, her Christian iconophilia, her American Holiness training, her cultural knowledge as a Newfoundlander, and all the other influences on her as a religious "American" to create individual objects of vernacular religious belief. Sister Ann is not merely a Newfoundland vernacular religious artist, nor even a Canadian one, but the epitome of the vernacular religious artist within the North American context. Her religious art expresses her encounter,

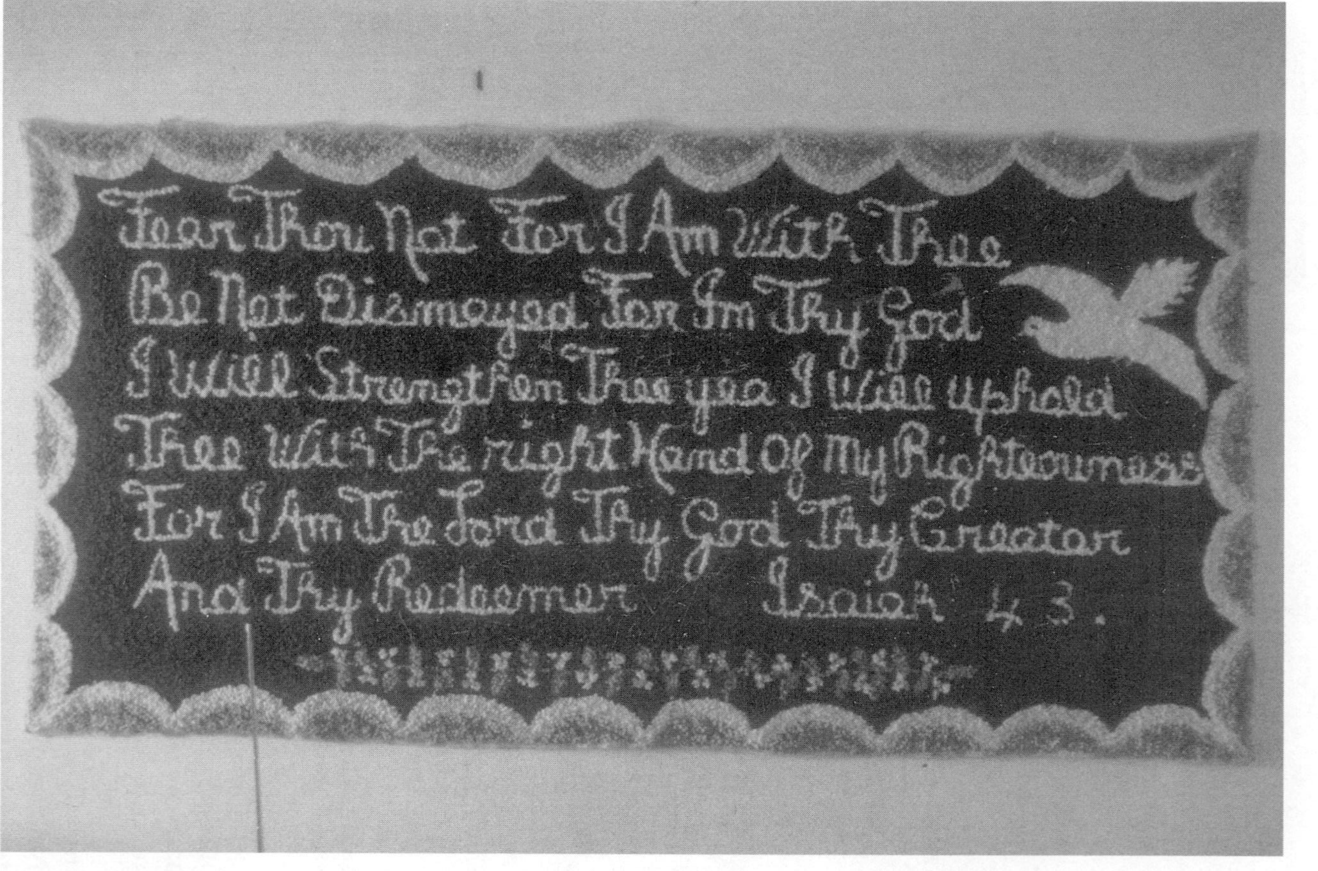

Figure 5. Fear Thou Not For I Am With Thee, n.d., 36 inches × 72 inches. Estate of Sister Ann Ameen. Photo, Leonard Norman Primiano.

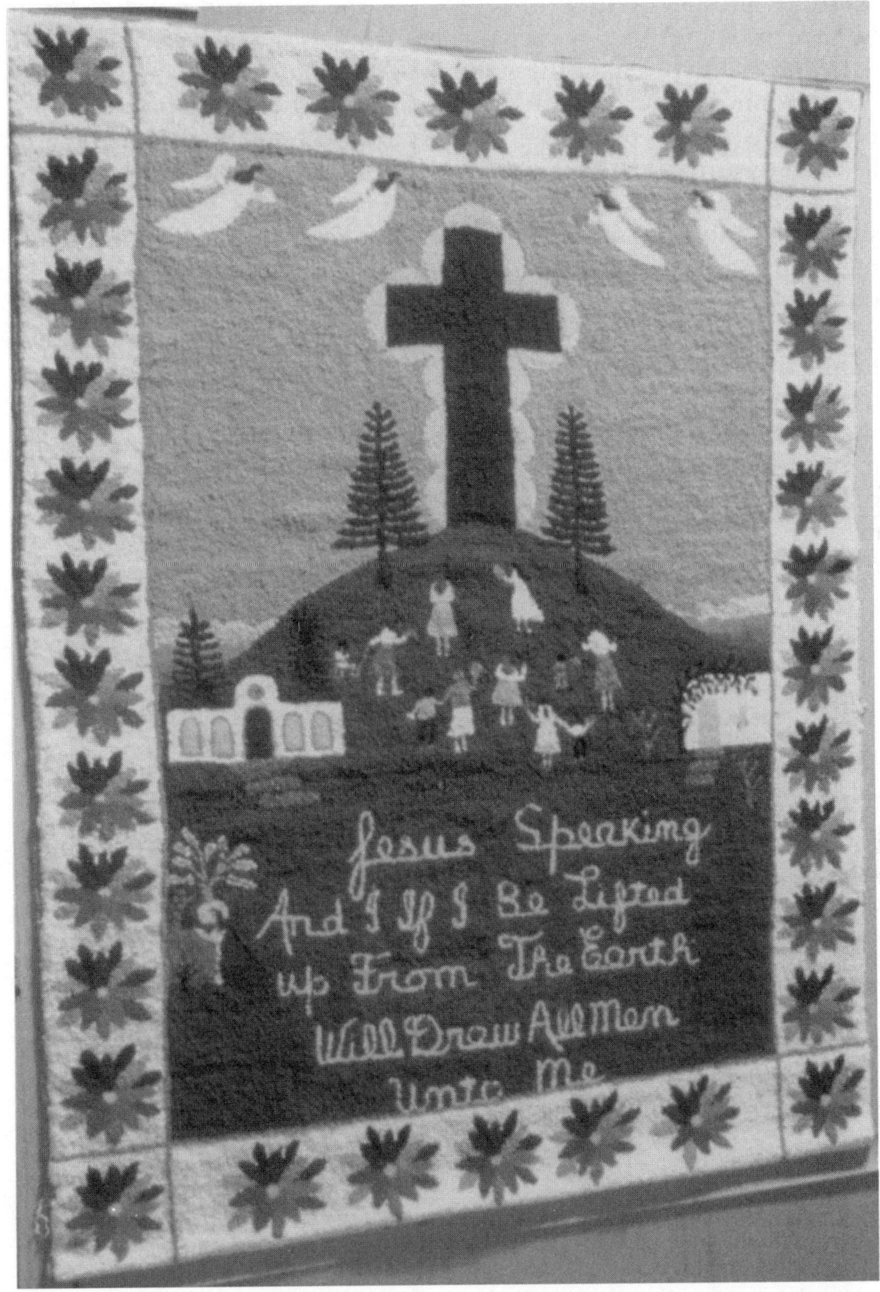

Figure 6. Jesus Speaks, 1983, 108 inches × 144 inches. Museum of Civilization, Ottawa. Photo, Museum of Civilization.

her contact, her exchange of religion, and ultimately her understanding and negotiation of religion as she lived and practiced it in
her everyday life.[31]

In the last five years of her life, when I would go to visit her cold
dusty home by the bay, she would speak of her intention to hook
more mats and to teach the technique to others. Such crafts could
be used to support the missionary work she saw as so essential. Alone
and seemingly abandoned by all but a few visitors, on several occasions she pulled—from a book which kept it flat—a color photocopy
of an image of Jesus from either a magazine or religious mailing. "I
would love to hook this picture," she would tell me. Sister Ann engaged in copy work, but who knows how her view of Jesus would have
finally materialized. She never was much of a copyist. Independent
to the end of her life, she lived in that private residence as long as
she could before entering a nursing home in 1997. There she died
in the company of some of her rugs. These individual expressions of
religion reflected the multitude of environments influential in their
creator's process of believing. Like Sister Ann Ameen, they embodied the textures of a religious life.

Notes

I would particularly like to thank the following individuals who assisted me in
the preparation of this article: Deborah Ann Bailey, Lourdes Barretto, Sharon Co-
chrane, Justin Falciani, Delf Hohmann, Diane E. Goldstein, Paul Smith, Philip His-
cock, Barbara Rieti, Douglas Thompson, Mary Thompson, Don Dempsey, Seth
Frechie, Ann Schwelm, Abel Rodriguez, Anne Jenner, and Lars Jenner. Peter Narváez introduced me to Sister Ann Ameen and has been incredibly generous with
his time and knowledge. Anne Budgell also introduced me to Sister Ann, has
warmly shared her own insights about this special woman, and kindly read a draft
of the article. Stephen George helped me with valuable bibliographic sources and
other information on Newfoundland. Barbara Mercer and John Mercer aided my
research with their voluminous knowledge of Newfoundland culture. Arthur Petten
and Joyce Petten graciously welcomed me into their home. The careful reading of
Charlie McCormick, my colleague at Cabrini College, was an enormous asset. Kath-
leen Malone O'Connor's perceptive comments on drafts of this article were also
invaluable.

1. Sources for the three introductory epigraphs are: 1) Sister Ann Ameen, *Leadings of the Holy Spirit*, 2:11. (This is a set of three pamphlets which Sister Ann had
privately published and which she sent out to various individuals. The volumes contain no stated date or publisher.) 2) Ecclesiasticus or the Wisdom of Jesus Son of
Sirach 38:34. 3) Henry Glassie, *The Spirit of Folk Art: The Girard Collection at the Museum of International Folk Art* (New York: Abrams, 1989), 42.

2. For definitional articles on vernacular religion, see Leonard Norman Primiano, "Vernacular Religion and the Search for Method in Religious Folklife," *Western Folklore* 54 (1995): 37–56; Leonard Norman Primiano, "Folk Religion," in *Folklore: An Encyclopedia of Beliefs, Customs, Tales, Music, and Art*, ed. Thomas A. Green (Santa Barbara, Calif.: ABC-CLIO, 1997), 710–17.

3. Christine Moeller and J. M. Sullivan wrote thoughtful appreciations of Sister Ann and her work at the time of her death. See Christine Moeller, "Newfoundland Treasure Lost," *Rug Hooking Guild of Newfoundland and Labrador Newsletter* 4, no. 1 (Spring 1998): 5, 7, plus unnumbered two-page insert; J. M. Sullivan, "Ann Sharpe Ameen Brown," *The Globe and Mail*, 23 April 1998, A24.

4. In Newfoundland, rugs are often referred to as "mats." A hooked or poked rug is a textile in which ripped or torn strips of cloth or yarn are forced through the meshing of a piece of burlap. A design drawn on the surface serves usually as the model for the desired image. For discussions of this tradition in Newfoundland, see Colleen Lynch, "The Fabric of Their Lives," in *The Fabric of Their Lives: Hooked and Poked Mats of Newfoundland and Labrador* (St. John's: The Art Gallery, Memorial University of Newfoundland, 1980); Gerald L. Pocius, "Hooked Rugs in Newfoundland: The Representation of Social Structure in Design," *Journal of American Folklore* 92 (1979): 273–84.

5. Sister Ann Ameen, *Leadings of the Holy Spirit*, 2:15.

6. Newfoundland joined the Canadian Confederation in 1949. The province of Newfoundland and Labrador is the most easterly of the Atlantic Provinces. It includes the island of Newfoundland, a number of smaller islands that surround it, and the enormous northern territory of Labrador which is connected to the Canadian mainland. When Newfoundlanders refer to "Newfoundland," they usually mean the island itself, as opposed to the province which includes Labrador.

7. The *Bay Roberts Guardian* had taken this article from a report in *The Montreal Gazette*.

8. Art historians David Morgan and Susan Promey have preferred to call such American artistic expressions the "Visual Culture of American Religions." See David Morgan and Sally M. Promey, *Exhibiting the Visual Culture of American Religions* (Valparaiso, Ind.: Brauer Museum of Art, Valparaiso University, 2000). American religious historian Colleen McDannell has referred to such material culture as "Material Christianity." See Colleen McDannell, *Material Christianity: Religion and Popular Culture in America* (New Haven: Yale University Press, 1995); see also Leonard Norman Primiano, "Review of Colleen McDannell, *Material Christianity: Religion and Popular Culture In America*," *The Records of the American Catholic Historical Society* 108 (1997): 83–87.

9. See Leonard Norman Primiano, "Post-Modern Sites of Catholic Sacred Materiality," in *Perspectives on American Religion and Culture*, ed. Peter W. Williams (New York: Blackwell, 1999), 187–202.

10. For a discussion of such terminology, see Roger Cardinal, "Toward an Outsider Aesthetic," in *The Artist Outsider: Creativity and the Boundaries of Culture*, ed. Michael D. Hall and Eugene W. Metcalf Jr. (Washington: Smithsonian Institution Press, 1994), 20–43. For a definition of "art brut," see Roger Cardinal, "Art brut," *Dictionary of Art* (New York: Macmillan, 1996), 2:515–16. For a definition of "naive art," see Roger Cardinal, "Naïve art," ibid., 439–42. The periodical *Raw Vision* offers a constellation of such terms each issue. See also folklorist Henry Glassie's re-

flections of art and folk art: "Folk Art," in *Folklore and Folklife: An Introduction*, ed. Richard M. Dorson (Chicago: University of Chicago Press, 1972), 253–80; *The Spirit of Folk Art: The Girard Collection at the Museum of International Folk Art* (New York: Abrams, 1989); *Material Culture* (Bloomington: Indiana University Press, 1999).

11. Charles G. Zug III, "Folk Art and Outsider Art: A Folklorist's Perspective," in *The Artist Outsider*, 151–52.

12. Joel and Kate Kopp, *American Hooked and Sewn Rugs: Folk Art Underfoot* (Albuquerque: University of New Mexico Press, 1995), 109.

13. Some Newfoundlanders recalled to me that Ameen did at times have young women who lived with her in St. John's assist with the hooking.

14. Lynch, "The Fabric of Their Lives," 12; see also Kopp, *American Hooked and Sewn Rugs*, 132–33.

15. So described by folklorist Jenny Michael in a personal communication.

16. Considerations of Squires and his work can be found in James Wade, "Gerald Leopold Squires," in *Dictionary of Newfoundland and Labrador Biography* (St. John's: Cuff, 1990), 323; see also Des Walsh and Susan Jamieson, *Gerald Squires, Newfoundland Artist* (St. John's: Breakwater Books, 1995).

17. Peter Gard, "Sister Act," *Canadian Art* (Spring 1994): 46–48.

18. Barbara Kirshenblatt-Gimblett, "Objects of Memory: Material Culture as Life Review," in *Folk Groups and Folklore Genres: A Reader*, ed. Elliott Oring (Logan: Utah State University Press, 1989).

19. Oring, ed., *Folk Groups and Folklore Genres*, 329.

20. For examinations of the ways the elderly shape memory projects and perform them before witnesses in the task of self-definition and life review, see Mary Hufford, *Chaseworld: Foxhunting and Storytelling in New Jersey's Pine Barrens* (Philadelphia: University of Pennsylvania Press, 1992); Mary Hufford, Marjorie Hunt, and Steven J. Zeitlin, *The Grand Generation: Memory, Mastery, Legacy* (Washington: Smithsonian Institution Traveling Exhibition Service; Seattle: University of Washington Press, 1987); Patrick Mullen, *Listening to Old Voices: Folklore, Life Stories, and the Elderly* (Bloomington: Indiana University Press, 1992); Barbara Myerhoff, *Number Our Days* (New York: Simon & Schuster, 1978).

21. Bruce Johnson, personal communication, September 1995.

22. Kirshenblatt-Gimblett, "Objects of Memory," 336.

23. Pocius, "Hooked Rugs in Newfoundland," 278. Pocius makes the point that rugs with geometric designs would be placed on the kitchen floor of Newfoundland homes for everyday family use, while more innovative patterns would be positioned on the front room floor where guests of a higher social status, such as clergy or merchants, were received (ibid., 274, 284).

24. Gerald L. Pocius, "Holy Pictures in Newfoundland Houses: Visual Codes for Secular and Supernatural Relationships," in *Media Sense: The Folklore-Popular Culture Continuum*, ed. Peter Narváez and Martin Laba (Bowling Green, Ohio: Bowling Green State University Press, 1986), 124–48. Gerald L. Pocius, *A Place to Belong: Community Order and Everyday Space in Calvert, Newfoundland* (Athens: University of Georgia Press, 1991).

25. Pocius explains the Newfoundland rug-hooking tradition as presenting "the extremes of stability and innovation, but instead of an individual making a choice between conformity (expressed in the use of geometric antecedents) and individuality (in the use of a unique antecedent), most women used both styles." See "Hooked Rugs in Newfoundland," 280–81.

26. See Philip and Sally Scharper, eds., *The Gospel in Art by the Peasants of Solentiname* (Maryknoll, N.Y.: Orbis Books, 1984).

27. Catherine L. Albanese, "Exchanging Selves, Exchanging Souls: Contact, Combination, and American Religious History," in *Retelling U.S. Religious History*, ed. Thomas A. Tweed (Berkeley: University of California Press, 1997), 203, 224.

28. When Albanese speaks of contact between religions, she is not limiting her discussion to contact between, for example, Christian denominations. She sees religious contact and exchange touching all religious communities within the American environment.

29. See Genevieve Lehr, "Anglican Church," *Encyclopedia of Newfoundland and Labrador*, 4 vols. (St. John's: Cuff, 1981) 1:48–51; David G. Pitt, "Methodism," ibid. (1991), 3:519–27; Burton K. James, "Pentecostal Assemblies of Newfoundland," ibid. (1993), 4:251–55; Raymond J. Lahey, "Roman Catholic Church," ibid., 622–31.

30. Bruce Johnson suggests that these landscapes, "although probably loosely based on actual places, are constructed scenes, places reinvented and improved upon by Sister Ann's imagination. Other than frequent references to rolling green hills, sea-birds, and the odd fishing trawler, these spaces are not necessarily indicative of Newfoundland . . . Sister Ann's landscapes are more aligned with the ideals of Arcadia or, more aptly, Eden—her imaginings ordered more by ideal and design than by reality." See Bruce Johnson, "Introduction," in *Faith and Works: The Hooked Mats of Sister Ann Ameen* (St. John's: Memorial University of Newfoundland, 1995), 6–7.

31. See also Albanese's study of her poet grandfather's rich artistic and religious life and his process of coming to religious belief. Catherine L. Albanese, *A Cobbler's Universe: Religion, Poetry, and Performance in the Life of a South Italian Immigrant* (New York: Continuum, 1997).

"And Art Shall Say, 'Let There Be Light' ": Religious Imagery and the Nineteenth-Century Musical Imagination

Annie Janeiro Randall
Bucknell University

IT is quite common to think of certain musical works such as Bach's fugues or Beethoven's symphonies as though they were sacred texts in which the "Commandments" of music are wondrously revealed anew at each performance. Composers of these sacred texts are accorded godlike or demigod status and are worshiped in the form of idealized marble busts or depicted as residing in a pantheon of the gods. The activities of their interpreters and explicators (conductors, instrumentalists, singers, theorists, historians) parallel those of the clergy and biblical scholars; musical study and performance are, in many ways, conceived as exercises in exegesis.

As in religion, music too has its fundamentalists: those whose interpretations claim to be based on the musical text alone or for whom the only valid version of a work is one proven to have come directly from the composer's own hand. Music historians and theorists are entrusted with preserving the holy texts and sacred objects for the study, use, and worship of future aspirants. Even the bodies of composers are exhumed; hair samples are snipped and fetishized in much the same way as saints' hair and clothing are made into holy relics.[1]

Musicians perform the sacred texts in ritual fashion, wearing black, as do religious orders, and subject themselves to grueling hours of disciplined music practice, comparable to the hours spent by religious acolytes kneeling in prayer or spent in careful scriptural study.[2] And like acolytes, aspiring musicians are led by a class of learned practitioners who hold the status of priests: the greater the skill and learning of our musical priests, the more likely he or she will ascend the hierarchy and be held in even greater esteem as a high priest or priestess, a master teacher or virtuoso performer of national or international repute. All members of the hierarchy are dedicated to revealing musical works to audiences whose reverential demeanor parallels that of congregations participating in a religious service. Music conservatories function as monasteries and convents, while in grandly conceived concert halls the central mystery of musical creation is reenacted with each performance of a sacred text .

This cryptoreligious sensibility is so embedded in the Western European art music tradition, so taken for granted, that it is rarely questioned even though it has much to do with the way we learn music, what music we are taught or not taught, how we perform music, and even what we listen to, how we listen to it, and what we derive from it. "Classical" music, cloaked in the garb of religion, claims for itself a privileged place among other cultural practices: it seems fair to ask why, when, and to what end religious imagery began to be used (and continues to be used) to describe acts of secular musical performance, composition, and appreciation. The midnineteenth century religion-saturated writings of Richard Wagner, Franz Liszt, Felix and Fanny Mendelssohn, and Carl Zelter were not the first or only ones to conceive musical practices in such terms, yet they are among the most influential because of the wide and lasting dissemination of their views.

Without question, Wagner's prose writings and operas offer not only the richest source of material on the topic of music and religion in the midnineteenth century but the most frequent and brazen use of religious language to describe his own work. In his operas, his "Art-works of the Future," Wagner's stated goal is to unite the "trinity" of music, dance, and poetry. In 1849, he wrote, "that each of the three partners, unlinked from the united chain and bereft thus of her own life and motion, can only carry on an artificially inbreathed and borrowed life;—not giving forth her sacred ordinances, as in their trinity."[3] In Wagner's operas, the composer reconstitutes the trinity, thus restoring its power to spiritually transform the listener.

Wagner's concept of the Artwork of the Future subsumes his formulation of the "Religion of the Future" and locates it as the historical heir to what he calls "Hellenic Religion." He exhorted his readers to:

look far hence to glorious Grecian Art, and gather from its inner understanding the outlines for the Art-work of the Future! . . . we have to stretch it out [Hellenic Religion] until its folds embrace the Religion of the Future, the Religion of *Universal Manhood,* and thus to gain already a presage of the Art-work of the Future . . . The Art-work is the living presentation of Religion . . . let us draw a bold and confident conclusion anent [*sic*] *the great and universal Art-work of the Future!*[4]

While this may sound like obvious hyperbole, as it did to some of Wagner's contemporaries (namely Brahms), the blending of music and religion powerfully influenced Wagner's generation and succeeding generations, skeptics like Nietzsche and Thomas Mann notwithstanding. Had Wagner's writings not been widely read, disseminated, and translated across Europe and North America, it would be tempting to lump his writings in with the similar rantings of Greek revivalists who periodically surface and disappear in the history of Western European art music.[5] But Wagner's critical writings were devoured by clubs of devoted Wagnerians: in Paris, the *Revue wagnérienne* was founded as an outlet for French literary responses to Wagner's music and aesthetics; in Italy, a similar journal, *Cronaca wagneriana,* circulated; and in England, the aptly named *The Meister* served as the chief purveyor of Wagnerism.[6]

Liszt's writings, like Wagner's, made audacious use of religious language, symbols, and images. Liszt actually took minor holy orders and in the last years of his profligate life wore priest's robes daily and for recitals. Numerous photographs and caricatures from this period show Liszt in the floor-length, high-collared habit of a Catholic clergyman. In 1835, fourteen years before Wagner published his *Art-work of the Future,* Liszt, while making no transhistorical claims for his music, simply asserted that religion was failing to do its job and that music would have to step into the breach:

Today, when the altar is cracked and tumbling, today, when pulpit and ceremonies have become objects of doubt and derision, art must emerge from the temple, must spread out and accomplish its far-reaching evolution outside.

As before, and to an even greater degree, music must seek out the PEOPLE and GOD, go from one to the other; improve, moralize, console man, bless and glorify God . . . *all classes of society,* finally, will merge in a common religious sentiment, grand and sublime.

And art shall say, "Let there be light."

May it come, may it come, therefore, this glorious era in which art shall fulfill itself by developing in all its aspects and rise to the highest level by uniting mankind in brotherhood by means of rapturous wonders.[7]

Published in the *Gazette musicale de Paris*, Liszt's articles reached a wide audience rather effortlessly due to his celebrity and international reputation as the foremost piano virtuoso of his day.

The idea that religion was failing to moralize, console man, and glorify God was also expressed by the composer and teacher Carl Zelter and Felix Mendelssohn in Berlin. Zelter, founder of the Berlin Singing Academy, and Felix Mendelssohn, the first director of the Leipzig Conservatory, are important in this discussion for at least two reasons: while Liszt and Wagner forged an indelible connection between music and religion in the public's mind via the newspapers and performing spaces of European capitals, the Mendelssohns and Zelter brought the religious sensibility to the sphere of music education and are largely responsible for institutionalizing it and embedding the idea of music as sacred text into the conservatory curriculum. Second, Zelter and the Mendelssohns were responsible for reviving J. S. Bach's music, rescuing it from obscurity, and successfully transferring his works from the church to the concert hall, thus beginning his secular deification. Fanny Mendelssohn, who was also centrally involved in the Bach revival, wrote, "I know of no preacher more insistent than old Bach, especially when he ascends the pulpit in an aria and holds onto his theme until he has utterly moved, edified and convinced his congregation."[8]

The Mendelssohn/Zelter performance of Bach's "St. Matthew Passion" at the Berlin Singakademie in 1829 can be considered the germination point for nineteenth-century musicoreligious perspectives on music after which the idea rapidly took root and flourished. On the significance of this performance, John Toews writes:

> this was not merely a priceless aesthetic legacy echoing a past world of metaphysical security and rational order, but contained as a kind of prophetic essence the foundations of a new national ethical consciousness . . . Although the St. Matthew Passion was performed in a neoclassical temple of art by lay musicians at a benefit concert for a ticket-holding, paying audience, both Fanny and Felix thought that the music had transformed the attenders of a secular concert into participants in a sacred service.[9]

The influence of these ideas on concert and conservatory life in Leipzig and Berlin is plain to see in light of the fact that the Mendelssohns' musical tastes were highly regarded in both cities: Fanny's choice of music for her Sunday musicales in Berlin was closely followed and imitated, while Felix's position as a conductor in Leipzig made his repertoire choices (and manner of presenting them to the public) highly influential.[10] Zelter and Mendelssohn, through their positions in music academies, were responsible for training the generation of musicians that left Germany after the 1848 upheavals and founded conservatories across Europe and in the United States. These musicians, as teachers, passed on the tradition and sensibilities of Zelter and Mendelssohn to their own students.

Zelter and Mendelssohn's goal, to "elevate music to the status of a 'high' art, directed toward the cultivation and expression of the universal, spiritual dimension of human existence"[11] was built upon the late eighteenth-century aesthetic foundation laid by Johann Joachim Winckelmann, Karl Philipp Moritz, Immanuel Kant, Johann Cristoph Friedrich von Schiller, Johann Gottfried Herder, Johann Gottlieb Fichte, Friedrich Wilhelm Joseph von Schelling, Wilhelm Heinrich Wackenroder, and Ludwig Tieck. Before the so-called aesthetic idealism of the turn of the century, it was common to think of music in concrete, functional terms: except for music that was specifically designed for religious worship, music was expected to be no more than sensually pleasing and agreeable. While it could be emotionally moving also, before the formulations of the aesthetic idealists gained currency, secular music was not yet considered a vehicle of spiritual transcendence. Without the intellectual framework offered in the publications of these writers, the religion-music link may not have taken root so deeply in the nineteenth-century imagination.

Zelter, the Mendelssohns, and their followers grafted their religious sensibility onto Wilhelm Wackenroder's concept of "the Ideal" in a work of music. Wackenroder held that music operates in the realm of the transcendent and is superior to other arts in its lack of resemblance to the "real" world. In the novella *Herzensergiessungen eines kunstliebenden Klosterbruders* (1797), he articulated this concept through the musical experiences of his protagonist:

> When Joseph was at a grand concert he seated himself in a corner, without so much as glancing at the brilliant assembly of listeners, and listened with precisely the same reverence as if he were in church—just as still and motionless, his eyes cast down to the floor. Not the slightest

sound escaped his notice, and his keen attention left him in the end quite limp and exhausted.[12]

Karl Dahlhaus comments:

> The "holy art of music" that sends Wackenroder-Berlinger [Joseph] into such religious transports is not church music but a symphony, and the location that causes him to feel "as if he were in church" is a concert hall. In other words, whereas music, in the form of church music, used to partake of religion as revealed in the "Word," it now, as autonomous music capable of conveying the "inexpressible," has become religion itself.[13]

This kind of thinking made it quite reasonable for the listener to posit a divine presence at the center of this "angelically pure art" (Wackenroder), and to imagine a musical performance to be a religious experience. This is exactly what the Mendelssohns, Zelter, and, later, Liszt and Wagner did, creating a powerfully seductive intellectual fashion and, at the same time, providing models for their followers. These appropriations of religious language, images, and symbols coincided with tremendously important developments in the spread of Western European art music: the founding of the world's major conservatories and performing organizations; an explosion in the number of periodicals about music; and a boom in the building of concert halls and music schools in cities of all sizes in the United States. Hence, the link between religion and art music became institutionalized by the founders of these establishments and even fueled a missionarylike zeal to create satellite institutions in their image.

It is interesting to speculate what would have become of the nineteenth century's musicoreligious sensibility had it not coincided with a dispersal of European musicians around the globe and had it not been refined and propagated as an ideology by the institutions that were founded upon its premises. Might it have run its course and died out as classicism did in the late eighteenth and early nineteenth centuries had it not become embedded in the performance practice, educational principles, and aesthetic orientation of these institutions? Given the nature of institutions and their inborn mechanisms for self-perpetuation, it is hardly surprising that the musicoreligious foundations upon which they were built continue to survive and shape the course of the Western European art music tradition.

Notes

1. The exhumation and scrutiny of what is believed to be Mozart's corpse periodically occupies the composer's devotees.

2. Ethnomusicologists have long recognized the similarities between religious and musical practices in the Western European art tradition. See Bruno Nettl, "Mozart and the Ethnomusicological Study of Western Culture," *Yearbook for Traditional Music* 21(1989): 1–16. See also Bruno Nettl, *Heartland Excursion: Ethnomusicological Reflections on Schools of Music* (Urbana: University of Illinois Press, 1995); Philip Bohlman, "Epilogue: Music and Its Canons," in *Disciplining Music: Musicology and Its Canons* (Chicago: University of Chicago Press, 1992), 197–210.

3. Richard Wagner, *Das Kunstwerk der Zukunft* (Leipzig: Wigand, 1849); printed in English as *The Artwork of the Future and Other Works*, trans. W. Ashton Ellis (Lincoln: University of Nebraska Press, 1993), 95.

4. Ibid., 90.

5. See, for instance, the works of Nicola Vicentino (ca. 1511–1572) in which the composer attempted to apply ancient Greek theoretical principles within a sixteenth-century musical idiom. In Henry W. Kaufmann, *The Life and Works of Nicola Vicentino* (Rome: American Institute of Musicology, 1996).

6. For a concise discussion of Wagnerism see Erwin Koppen, "Wagnerism as Concept and Phenomenon," in *Wagner Handbook*, ed. Ulrich Müller, Peter Wapnewski, and John Deathridge (Cambridge: Harvard University Press, 1992), 353.

7. Jean Chantavoine, ed., *Franz Liszt: Pages romantiques* (Paris: Alcan, 1912), 65–67; excerpted in *Music in the Western World: A History in Documents*, ed. Piero Weiss and Richard Taruskin, trans. Piero Weiss (New York: Schirmer, 1984), 366–67.

8. Fanny Mendelssohn Hensel, quoted in *The Letters of Fanny Mendelssohn Hensel*, ed. and trans. Marcia Citron (New York: Pendragon Press, 1987), 160–61. See also Michael Marissen, "Religious Aims in Mendelssohn's 1829 Berlin-Singakademie Performances of Bach's St. Matthew Passion," *Musical Quarterly* 77 (1993): 718–26.

9. John Toews, "Memory and Gender in the Remaking of Fanny Mendelssohn's Musical Identity: The Chorale in *Das Jahr*," *Musical Quarterly* 77 (1993): 729.

10. For detailed treatment of Felix Mendelssohn's influence in Leipzig see Sieghart Döhring, "Dresden and Leipzig: Two Bourgeois Centers," in *The Early Romantic Era*, ed. Alexander Ringer (Englewood Cliffs, N.J.: Prentice Hall, 1990), 149–56.

11. Toews, "Memory and Gender," 733.

12. W. H. Wackenroder, quoted in Carl Dahlhaus, *Nineteenth-Century Music*, trans. J. Bradford Robinson (Berkeley: University of California Press, 1989), 94.

13. Ibid.

Rebuilding Babel:
Science, Fiction, and a New Divinity

John Rickard
Bucknell University

Man has . . . become a kind of prosthetic God.
—Sigmund Freud, *Civilization and Its Discontents*

I would rather be a cyborg than a goddess.
—Donna J. Haraway, "A Cyborg Manifesto"

THE paradigmatic tale of God's punishment of humans for overreaching with technology is the story of the Tower of Babel in Genesis. In this story, human beings, who communicate in one common language, decide to build "a city and a tower, whose top may reach unto heaven; and let us make us a name, lest we be scattered abroad upon the face of the whole earth." God's response is not encouraging: "Behold, the people is one, and they have all one language; and this they begin to do: and now nothing will be restrained from them, which they have imagined to do." As punishment for their pride, God decides to "confound the language of all the earth" and scatter the people across the earth (Gen. 11: 4–9).

The sense of a divinely determined boundary or limit to human science and technological development runs through much of our writing and thinking about these issues. Especially in what we have come to call science fiction, a clear pattern was established early in the history of the genre in which humans who took on the roles and powers traditionally ascribed to God in Jewish and Christian theology inevitably failed and were horribly punished. One of the earliest and clearest examples of such cautionary fictions is Mary Shelley's *Frankenstein, or The Modern Prometheus,* in which the tale of an overreaching scientist attempting to create human life is couched in highly religious language, especially in the later 1831 edition. Shelley turned to religious paradigms in order to express her anxiety concerning the possibilities held out by the new scientific discoveries of her day. Shelley's antihero, Dr. Frankenstein, attempts to take upon himself the godlike power of creating a new species, yearning to "break through" the "ideal bounds" of life and death in order to become the "creator and source" of a "new species,"[1] but he finds himself unequal to the task and is punished for his pride and inadequacy. Shelley continually draws parallels between the scientist Frankenstein and the great rebels against divinity, Prometheus and Satan. The traditional religious paradigm is embodied in the newly created "monster," who addresses his creator in the antique language of thee and thou reserved, by Shelley's time, for religious discourse: " 'Remember, that I am thy creature; I ought to be thy Adam; but I am rather the fallen angel, whom thou drivest from joy for no misdeed.' "[2] As a result of his prideful and ill-considered attempt to usurp the place of God within creation, the scientist Frankenstein becomes the slave of his own creation, losing everything he loves.

Another example of a cautionary tale about the dangers of scientific ambition is H. G. Wells's *The Island of Dr. Moreau* (1896), which again portrays the scientist in the role of a dysfunctional god.[3] Like Frankenstein, Wells's Moreau attempts to create new species and in doing so quite consciously takes on a godlike role. We can see this role reflected in Wells's parodies of religious law and ritual in the novel, especially in the pathetic and degraded recitations of "the Law," which Moreau has inculcated in the Beast People he has created in order to keep them from reverting to their animal pasts:

> Not to go on all Fours; *that* is the Law. Are we not Men?
> Not to suck up Drink; *that* is the Law. Are we not Men?
> Not to eat Flesh nor Fish; *that* is the Law. Are we not Men?
> Not to claw Bark of Trees; *that* is the Law. Are we not Men?
> Not to chase other Men; *that* is the Law. Are we not Men?
>
> . . . .
>
> *His* is the House of Pain.
> *His* is the Hand that makes.
> *His* is the Hand that wounds.
> *His* is the Hand that heals.[4]

Moreau, like Frankenstein, sets himself up in the role of a god over a creation he cannot control, and like Frankenstein, he is destroyed by this creation.

Of course, one could cite many other examples of such cautionary tales of the punishment of the human scientist for the misuse of science and technology, and such dystopian fictions of retribution for human hubris are still being produced, from *The Terminator* (1984) to *Jurassic Park* (1993). In recent years, however, one can also identify a significant change in the way the theme of the scientific manipulation of life is handled. In much recent writing we find a new, more optimistic or utopian treatment of these themes developing, not only in science fiction but within public discourse as well. In these newer works, one senses that the emotional or tonal tide has turned, and we can now find a body of work that suggests that human beings can or even should embrace technology and the technologization of the human body in an attempt to evolve self-consciously into a new species and even to constitute ourselves as a new divinity, to move into the gap opened by the death of the old divinity. Contemporary fiction and film have increasingly come to embrace the notion of posthuman evolution, of the acquisition—usually through technological prostheses—of godlike powers of omniscience, omnipresence, and immortality. In such fictional and nonfictional writing, one could suggest, we are indeed rebuilding Babel, seemingly secure in the sense that we are climbing into a vacant space now devoid of a punishing God.[5]

The shift in paradigms I am describing here is of course a large-scale phenomenon with many possible causes, but I think it is clear that in our culture the notion of "playing God" is losing some of its negative connotations, for better or worse, as we become more resigned to the inevitability of genetic engineering, cloning, and other human incursions into the creation and manipulation of species, including our own species. Undoubtedly, the impetus for much of this recent writing can be traced back to Darwin's uncoupling of the human and the divine through evolutionary theory, which implied a new instability in the human form, a form created not by a careful, divine Designer, but rather by a blind, even random, natural process. This sense of instability is coupled, in the final paragraph of *The Descent of Man,* with an optimistic view of the human species that includes both the "lowly origin" of humanity and the possibility of a godlike future:

> Man may be excused for feeling some pride at having risen, though not
> through his own exertions, to the very summit of the organic scale; and
> the fact of his having thus risen, instead of having been aboriginally

> placed there, may give him hope for a still higher destiny in the distant
> future . . . We must, however, acknowledge . . . that man with all his noble
> qualities . . . with his god-like intellect which has penetrated into the
> movements and constitution of the solar system—with all these exalted
> powers—Man still bears in his bodily frame the indelible stamp of his
> lowly origin.[6]

Many other cultural sources for the emergence of the "posthuman"
trend I am examining here exist, among them Friedrich Nietzsche,
who in the wake of Darwin imagined a radical break between the
past and future of the species, proclaiming in *The Will to Power* that
"I write for a species that does not yet exist: for the 'masters of the
earth.' "[7] Nietzsche's ideas concerning the death of God, the birth
of the overman, and the consequent need to rethink our place and
role in the cosmos ultimately require a need to transcend humanity
as it now exists, for as Nietzsche's madman exclaims in *The Gay Science*, "God is dead. God remains dead. And we have killed him . . .
Must we ourselves not become gods simply to appear worthy of it?
There has never been a greater deed; and whoever is born after us—
for the sake of this deed he will belong to a higher history than all
history hitherto."[8]

Sigmund Freud took Nietzsche's thinking about the continued
evolution of humanity a step further in *Civilization and Its Discontents*,
where he ties the cultural and technological evolution of the human
body to the diminishing need for God. Arguing that "with every tool
man is perfecting his own organs, whether motor or sensory, or is
removing the limits to their functioning,"[9] Freud provides a catalogue of the technological extension of human organs by means of
technology (the telescope as an extension of the eye, the telephone
as an extension of the ear, the photograph as an extension of memory, and so on). As an athiest, Freud explains that the need for gods
declines as human power (if not human happiness) grows through
technological development. "Long ago," Freud argues, man

> formed an ideal conception of omnipotence and omniscience which he
> embodied in his gods. To these gods he attributed everything that
> seemed unattainable to his wishes, or that was forbidden to him. One
> may say, therefore, that these gods were cultural ideals. To-day he has
> come very close to the attainment of this ideal, he has almost become a
> god himself.

In this striking passage Freud concludes that "man has, as it were,
become a kind of prosthetic God. When he puts on all his auxiliary

organs he is truly magnificent, but those organs have not grown on to him and they still give him much trouble at times. Nevertheless, he is entitled to console himself with the thought that this development will not come to an end precisely with the year 1930 A.D."[10]

Recent developments in computerized electronic technology, global information systems, and biomedical technologies have not perfected human life, of course, and Freud's question of whether our technological innovations make us happier than those who lived before us is still as compelling and unanswerable as it was in 1929, when he wrote *Civilization and Its Discontents.* Nonetheless, the speed with which our culture has extended the technological "prostheses" Freud discusses has led to an increasing utopianism in the ways we imagine ourselves in a transition beyond the human into a virtual godhood. Many contemporary science fiction novels, films, and stories, in fact, seem to imply that this difficult fit between the human body and its technological prostheses has become easier, and the conviction that we are on the verge of a momentous transformation into something new and strange or that this transformation has already occurred seems to pervade our fictions and our hopes for ourselves. Contemporary writers, unlike Mary Shelley or H. G. Wells, are now inclined routinely to imagine new, virtually perfected human states without the sense of trangression and punishment attendant upon earlier treatments of the technological control of evolution. These writers are reimagining humankind—or as it is now fashionably called, posthumanity—transformed through this technology into prosthetic gods. Suddenly, we find that writers are intent on rebuilding Babel, as it were, envisioning a new, godlike human race in which individuals have the power to disembody and extend themselves almost infinitely.

Arthur C. Clarke's *2001: A Space Odyssey,* published in 1968, is a relatively early example, ending with the image of a new human race, transfigured and given godlike powers as the result of its contact—through space technology—with alien intelligence. At the end of this book (and film), the human being named David Bowman (now "an entity who had called himself David Bowman") becomes something new and different, which Clarke images as a cosmic child or "star child." Here he is returned to the Earth to take his place as the new "god" who will now begin the next phase of human evolution:

> There before him, a glittering toy no Star-Child could resist, floated the planet Earth with all its peoples.

He had returned in time. Down there on that crowded globe, the alarms would be flashing across the radar screens, the great tracking telescopes would be searching the skies—and history as men knew it would be drawing to a close.

A thousand miles below, he became aware that a slumbering cargo of death had awoken, and was stirring sluggishly in its orbit. The feeble energies it contained were no possible menace to him; but he preferred a cleaner sky. He put forth his will, and the circling megatons flowered in a silent detonation that brought a brief, false dawn to half the sleeping globe.

Then he waited, marshaling his thoughts and brooding over his still untested powers. For though he was master of the world, he was not quite sure what to do next.

But he would think of something.[11]

Much recent science fiction envisions a near-future in which human beings will evolve into the ether of the virtual world being created by computers. The prosthetic possibilities of computer technology are already stunning, and these books, by authors such as William Gibson, Neil Stephenson, Pat Cadigan, and others imagine a world—certainly not always a pleasant one—in which we will be able to "jack in" to a world-wide computer network or cyberspace (Stephenson calls it a "metaverse" in *Snow Crash*) where we will have almost limitless potential for extension and where we will coexist with and meld into vast and powerful new forms of consciousness in the form of artificial intelligences. Such fantasies imagine again a godlike power for human beings who, by extending their psyches into cyberspace, move beyond the human and achieve a previously unimaginable potential for power and knowledge. The ultimate fantasy of such fictions is "uploading," based upon the idea that as computer technology becomes more sophisticated and as attempts to create "artificial intelligences" bear fruit, it will be possible to leave the body ("the meat") behind and "upload" one's psyche—memories, personality, and all—into an evolving, intelligent, and electronic world-mind of sorts.

Gibson's vision of the future in *Neuromancer* is a dark one, clouded by sinister technologies and the possibility of life beyond death within them.[12] Gibson's character Dixie Flatline is a computer hacker whose intelligence has been preserved after his death in a "construct" that allows him to converse and scheme with Case, the book's protagonist; like Petronius' Sibyl cited in the epigram to T. S. Eliot's *The Waste Land,* he wants only to die, to be relieved from his disembodied halflife. In contrast, an *X-Files* episode entitled "Kill Switch," written by Gibson and Tom Maddox and aired in 1998, views the idea of uploading and merging one's consciousness with artificial intelligence more positively. In this made-for-television story, computer hacker Esther Nairn and her lover, like Frankenstein and Dr. Moreau before them, have participated in the creation of a new life form—an artificial intelligence which has become sentient by evolving on the internet. Esther's desire is to "upload" herself into the artificial intelligence, or AI. As she explains it to Dana Scully, the FBI detective who has arrested her: "Uploading . . . transfer of memory, of consciousness to the distributed system maintained by the AI. Imagine being mingled so completely with another that you no longer need your physical self" ("Kill Switch").[13] At the end of the episode, Nairn's body has been destroyed by the AI, but it appears that she has also been granted her wish of being uploaded into a new form of consciousness.

Perhaps the most intriguing fantasy of disembodiment and power is "True Names," a story by Vernor Vinge published in 1981. In "True Names," Vinge imagines an avatar-based cyberspace—in other words, an internet in which people can create three-dimensional icons to represent themselves and experience themselves moving through a virtual world, interacting with others. Vinge's protagonist is a writer and computer hacker named Roger Pollack who goes by the name of Mr. Slippery in the Other Plane, the virtual world that the internet has become in Vinge's fiction—a virtual world in which disembodied human (and nonhuman) inhabitants can choose fanciful and shifting shapes to represent themselves and yet a world that is intricately connected to the "real world" of satellites, governments, and weapons systems. Mr. Slippery and his friend Erythrina— two powerful computer hackers—become involved in an investigation of a shadowy and nefarious presence that is working to establish control of the world's information systems and, at the climax of the story, find themselves in a battle with this villain, again not a human being but, it turns out, another artificial intelligence. Mr. Slippery finds that, with his mind out of his body and able to access a wide array of computers, satellites, and other information technologies, he does indeed become a prosthetic god. As Mr. Slippery and Erythrina take on more and more power in conducting a cosmic battle with the AI, Vinge imagines what it would be like to have the ability to distribute oneself throughout the global network of electronics we have created, to have a godlike omniscience and virtual omnipo-

tence, to use what we are now calling the internet as a prothesis for
the central nervous system:

> Erythrina's voice was faint against the roar, *"Use everything, not just the
> inputs!"* And he had just enough sense left to see what she meant. He
> controlled more than raw data now; if he could master them, the conti-
> nent's computers could process this avalanche, much the way parts of
> the human brain preprocess their input. More seconds passed, but now
> with a sense of time, as he struggled to distribute his very consciousness
> through the System.
>
> Then it was over, and he had control once more. But things would
> never be the same: the human that had been Mr. Slippery was an insect
> wandering in the cathedral his mind had become. There simply was
> more there than before. No sparrow could fall without his knowledge,
> via air traffic control; no check could be cashed without his noticing over
> the back communication net. More than three hundred million lives
> swept before what his senses had become.[14]

Like Clarke's "star child" in *2001*, Mr. Slippery finds that his status
as prosthetic god has given him a new perspective on the Earth, one
never before available to a human being:

> Mr. Slippery looked around him, using all his millions of perceptors.
> The Earth floated serene. Viewed in the visible, it looked like a thousand
> pictures he had seen as a human. But in the ultraviolet, he could follow
> its hydrogen aura out many thousands of kilometers. And the high-en-
> ergy detectors on satellites at all levels perceived the radiation belts in
> thousands of energy levels, oscillating in the solar wind. Across the
> oceans of the world, he could feel the warmth of the currents, see just
> how fast they were moving . . . Every ship in the seas, every aircraft now
> making for safe landing, every one of the loans, the payments, the meals
> of an entire race registered clearly on some part of his consciousness.
> With perception came power; almost everything he saw, he could alter,
> destroy, or enhance. By the analogical rules of the covens, there was only
> one valid word for themselves in their present state: they were gods.[15]

After Mr. Slippery and Erythrina defeat the AI, they voluntarily
choose to withdraw themselves from the network and give up their
power. When the two finally meet for the first time in the flesh, Pollack discovers that Erythrina, whose avatar represents her as a beautiful young woman, is really an aged woman named Deborah Char-
teris. Here, she reveals that while she had the power to extend
herself throughout the system, she managed to upload her personal-

ity and memory into it so that when her body dies, part of her will remain within the system:

> She was grinning now, an open though conspiratorial grin that was very familiar. "When Bertrand Russell was very old, and probably as dotty as I am now, he talked of spreading his interests and attention out to the greater world and away from his own body, so that when that body died he would scarcely notice it, his whole consciousness would be so diluted through the outside world.
>
> "For him, it was wishful thinking, of course. But not for me. My kernel is out here in the System. Every time I'm there, I transfer a little more of myself. The kernel is growing into a true Erythrina, who is also truly me. When this body dies . . . *I* will still be, and you can still talk to me."
>
> . . . for an instant, Pollack came near to understanding things that had once been obvious. Processors kept getting faster, memories larger. What now took a planet's resources would someday be possessed by everyone. Including himself.[16]

Many other contemporary fictions imagine such transformations of the self into data through computerized protheses. In Neil Stephenson's 1993 novel *Snow Crash,* for example, he incorporates the myth of Babel directly into the plot of the novel, theorizing that the original human language functioned much like the machine language that underlies all computer software—the fundamental, binary language of zeroes and ones used as the basis for all computer programming. Stephenson's novel depends on a clever analogy between computer hardware and the central nervous system: the "snow crash" of the title is a computer virus that infects not only the user's computer, but also moves into the nervous system, reducing affected human beings to an incomprehensible babble, human machine language. Stephenson views religions as viruses—like computer viruses—that aggressively move from host to host, infecting them with their ideologies and thus replicating themselves. In *Snow Crash,* the virus is a dangerous force that reduces humans to irrationality and to the human machine language that existed before Babel; just as computer languages such as COBOL and C + + overlay and make sense of machine language, so English, Hindi, and other human languages have come to overlay and rationalize the original language of Eden. Stephenson's protagonist, aptly named Hiro Protagonist, finally suggests that "maybe Babel was the best thing that ever happened to us."[17] Stephenson's book, like Vinge's story, finally envisions a refusal of a conversion to a purely digital state, but in its acceptance of a parallel between human mental structure and computer hardware and software, it also suggests that we hover on the verge of such a merger of human and machine.

The rapid—Stephenson might say viral—proliferation of this theme of posthuman or transhuman evolution is by no means limited only to fiction. Just as Charles Darwin, Friedrich Nietzsche, and Sigmund Freud in many ways stimulated the cultural fantasy I have been describing, contemporary theorists continue to speculate on the potential effects of our transformation from humans to posthumans or, as Donna J. Haraway puts it, cyborgs. Haraway's important and very influential essay "A Cyborg Manifesto: Science, Technology, and Socialist-Feminism in the Late Twentieth Century" argues that "we are all chimeras, theorized and fabricated hybrids of machine and organism; in short, we are cyborgs."[18] In a complex exploration of the possible meanings of this transformation, Haraway significantly contrasts this new posthuman identity with the traditional origin of humanity in the Garden of Eden: "The cyborg would not recognize the Garden of Eden; it is not made of mud and cannot dream of returning to dust."[19] "There are several consequences," Haraway argues,

> to taking seriously the imagery of cyborgs as other than our enemies. Our bodies, ourselves; bodies are maps of power and identity. Cyborgs are no exception. A cyborg body is not innocent; it was not born in a garden; it does not seek unitary identity and so generate antagonistic dualisms without end (or until the world ends); it takes irony for granted . . . The machine is not an it to be animated, worshipped, and dominated. The machine is us, our processes, an aspect of our embodiment. We can be responsible for machines; they do not dominate or threaten us. We are responsible for boundaries; we are they.[20]

Finally, for Haraway, embracing cyborg imagery "can suggest a way out of the maze of dualisms in which we have explained our bodies and our tools to ourselves. This is a dream not of a common language, but of a powerful infidel heteroglossia . . . I would rather be a cyborg than a goddess."[21]

These various fantasies of human transformation are mirrored extensively on the internet in many sites devoted to "transhumanism" or "posthumanism": to the proposition of directed evolution beyond the human, to the replacement of God by the posthuman, to cyborg culture and the supposed possibility of uploading oneself into machinery within the near future. These sites around the world present surprising (at least, for me) evidence that there are human beings actively planning to rebuild Babel (if that is one way we wish to look at it), to transgress—as much as it may actually be possible—the boundaries that in the past proved so daunting to writers such as Mary Shelley and H. G. Wells. Perhaps the most provocative of these writers on the internet is one Max More, President of the Extropy Institute (www.extropy.org) and author of a number of transhuman declarations and manifestos. In "On Becoming Posthuman" (1994), More begins with an epigraph from Nietzsche ("I teach you the overman. Man is something that is to be overcome. What have you done to overcome him?"), and ends with a rousing call to arms:

> *No one* will punish us for opening Pandora's box, for equipping ourselves with wings of posthuman intelligence and agelessness. Our old myths, holding us back from radical innovation, were adaptive in our early history, when we lived on the edge of extinction . . . Yes, we need to step carefully in modifying our brain function, our genes, and our physiology, but let us not hold back out of fear or false reverence for Nature as we find it.
>
> God was a primitive notion invented by superstitious people, people only just beginning to step out of ignorance and unconsciousness. The concept of God has been oppressive: a being more powerful than we, but made in the image of our crude self-conceptions. Our own process of endless progression into higher forms should and will replace this religious idea. Humanity is a temporary stage along the evolutionary pathway. We are not the zenith of nature's development. It is time for us to consciously take charge of ourselves and to accelerate our transhuman progress.
>
> No more gods, no more faith, no more timid holding back. Let us blast out of our old forms, our ignorance, our weakness, and our mortality. The future belongs to posthumanity.[22]

Clearly, much has changed since Mary Shelley's Frankenstein incurred the most horrible punishments for trangressing the boundaries of the human and daring to take upon himself the powers previously reserved for God. While much contemporary fiction and journalism still resonates with Shelley's warnings about human beings "playing God," a brave new world is taking shape in the form of visions of human transformation and posthuman existence in a universe populated by newly godlike humans. In this essay, I have tried to comment briefly, as an observer and a participant in the culture I am describing, upon a large cultural paradigm shift, a perceived evolutionary movement through technology into a new divinity. These developments, both in fiction and in nonfictional writing, show that we see our technology as more and more a part of ourselves and, correspondingly, see ourselves as malleable, manipulable, and virtually limitless. Whether such speculations are healthy, whether they are overoptimistic or even dystopian, and whether they ignore important questions of social justice at the expense of fantasies and the accumulation of power by the rich and developed nations of the world are all important questions beyond the scope of this short and general piece. What interests me here is the suggestion that many of us now perceive ourselves as a new species, as godlike creatures moving beyond the body into a new world where Babel can be rebuilt without incurring God's wrath.

Notes

1. Mary Shelley, *Frankenstein, or The Modern Prometheus*, ed. M. K. Joseph (New York: Oxford University Press, 1969), 54.

2. Ibid., 100.

4. H. G. Wells, *The Island of Dr. Moreau* (New York: Penguin Books, 1988), 59.

5. There is a large and growing body of literature on the question of trans- or posthumanity, and I am not attempting, in this brief and general overview, to address or respond to this work in detail. Interested readers may want to investigate further by examining such works as N. Katherine Hayles's *How We Became Posthuman: Virtual Bodies in Cybernetics, Literature, and Informatics* (Chicago: University of Chicago Press, 1999) or *Posthuman Bodies*, ed. Judith Halberstam and Ira Livingston (Bloomington: Indiana University Press, 1995).

6. Charles Darwin, *Darwin: A Norton Critical Edition*, ed. Philip Appleman, 2d ed. (New York: Norton, 1979).

7. Friedrich Nietzsche, *The Will to Power*, trans. Walter Kaufmann and R. J. Hollingdale (New York: Vintage Books, 1967), sec. 958.

8. Friedrich Nietzsche, *The Gay Science*, trans. Walter Kaufmann (New York: Vintage Books, 1974), sec. 125.

9. Sigmund Freud, *Civilization and Its Discontents*, ed. and trans. James Strachey (New York: Norton, 1989), 43.

10. Ibid., 44.

11. Arthur C. Clarke, *2001: A Space Odyssey* (New York: New American Library, 1982), 220–21.

12. William Gibson, *Neuromancer* (New York: Ace Books, 1984).

13. William Gibson and Tom Maddox, "Kill Switch," *The X-Files*. Dir. Rob Bowman. FOX. 15 February 1998.

14. Vernor Vinge, "True Names," in *Visions of Wonder: The Science Fiction Research*

Association Anthology, ed. David G. Hartwell and Milton T. Wolf (New York: Tor, 1996), 765.

15. Ibid., 773.

16. Ibid., 789–90.

17. Neil Stephenson, *Snow Crash* (New York: Bantam Books, 1992), 279.

18. Donna J. Haraway, "A Cyborg Manifesto," *Simians, Cyborgs, and Women: The Reinvention of Nature* (New York: Routledge, 1991).

19. Ibid., 151.

20. Ibid., 180.

21. Ibid., 181.

22. Max More, "On Becoming Posthuman" (1994), <www.maxmore.com/becoming.html>.

"I'd Rather Light a Candle Than Curse Your Darkness": Bringing Religion to Light in *Raising Arizona*

Eric Michael Mazur
Bucknell University

IN 1987 Joel and Ethan Coen released their second feature film, *Raising Arizona*, to mixed reviews. Hailed by some as a technical triumph, the movie was generally disregarded for its interpretive merit, and few movie analysts—neither those who enjoyed the film nor those who did not—considered its content or structure too deeply, suggesting that it was "just" a comedy. This was particularly true of scholars of religion and film who, despite some of the film's marketing,[1] did not consider it worthy of religious analysis. Consistent with an apparent tradition of overlooking the genre of comedy in the scholarly study of religion and film, up until now *Raising Arizona* has not received serious consideration.[2]

But this film is more than just another screwball comedy. From the large gold *chai* dangling around the neck of prison counselor "Doc Schwartz," to the constant biblical references throughout the narration, the story seems worthy of attention for its religious significance. Just as importantly, as a product of its era, it is also a reflection of the role and status of religion in late twentieth-century American society. Narrated like a personal confession, this film presents a classic story of a man caught between the desire to do good and the temptation to do evil, following the model of a morality play that is centuries old.[3] "The morality play," observes David Bevington, "tells the story of a representative individual Christian." It chooses a universal central figure who is surrounded "by abstract representations of his state of mind or body: Despair, Courage, Strength, Five Wits, and so on. He is counseled by his Good Angel and tempted by his Evil Angel, or by similar figures. Accordingly," Bevington concludes, "allegory is central to the method of the morality play."[4] *Raising Arizona* may not employ characters as explicitly identified as Temptation or Evil, but they are clearly part of the narrative structure. As such, this film can be understood as a modern morality play. And yet, given the role of religion in contemporary America, it is no surprise that—with a viewing audience less and less familiar with the religious texts upon which this story is modeled— the religious nuances of *Raising Arizona*, and films like it, have, in the words of Herbert Gans, gone "in one eye and out the other."[5]

Man in Search of Salvation:
The Religious Structure of *Raising Arizona*

"My name is H. I. McDunnough. Call me Hi."[6] With these words—reminiscent of the opening from Melville's *Moby Dick*—we meet Herbert I. McDunnough (Nicholas Cage), the narrator and central character of *Raising Arizona*. McDunnough is the classic Everyman; he's human, likable (even his nickname, "Hi," is familiar and inviting), and not perfect by any means, but not necessarily entirely corrupt. He's a good-hearted yet unsuccessful petty criminal who finds himself in and out of prison and who aspires to be decent while recognizing his own true nature—refusing, for example, to use a loaded gun in his repeated robbery attempts because he "didn't want to hurt anyone." Apparently still young at heart (he sports a Woody Woodpecker tattoo), as he relates the story of his own search for salvation, our modern Ishmael reveals both an underdeveloped folk wisdom and a manner of speaking that is both charming and affected in the way that the sixteenth-century King James translation of the Bible is to the modern reader.[7] This out-of-place manner is appropriate, as he is a man who has lost his way— not just because of his own simplemindedness or moral failings but because of the environment in which he is forced to function. He notes that he had "tried to stand up and fly straight, but it wasn't easy with that sumbitch Reagan in the White House." "I dunno," he continues, "they say he's a decent man, so maybe his advisors are confused." McDunnough is himself a decent man, but he, too, has been led astray by advisors—primarily his fellow men who, in a culture of ambiguity, fail to provide for him a moral compass.[8] For McDunnough, the world is a regular experience of struggle and oppression. Whether he is in prison or a free man, he is constantly battling the forces of the world around him, forces that never seem to give him a break and that seem determined to destroy him. As he notes about his frequent returns to prison, "I don't know how you come down on the incarceration question, whether it's for rehabilitation or revenge, but I was beginning to think revenge is the only argument makes any sense." Recounting his struggles in a narrative voice that implies he has survived his ordeal, McDunnough presents this phase of his life as a moral wandering. It is only appropriate that, during one of his many stints in prison, he listens as one of his cellmates (identified only in the screenplay as Moses) recounts an experience from his own youth ("An' when they was no meat we ate fowl. An' when they was no fowl we ate crawdad. An' when there was no crawdad to be foun, we ate san'."), sounding like the Hebrews as they crossed the Sinai desert and wandered in the wilderness. McDunnough is a seeking soul lost in the moral desert of the American southwest, and the only Moses he has to lead him to the promised land is in the bunk above him.

The cycle of crime and punishment in McDunnough's life is broken when he meets Edwinna "in the county lockup in Tempe, Arizona; a day I'll never forget." "Ed" (Holly Hunter) is a police officer responsible for booking arrested criminals and therefore a character with whom Hi has regular contact. Through a series of incarcerations, McDunnough flirts with Ed, consoling her when her fiancé leaves her for a cosmetologist ("who knew how to ply her feminine wiles"), inquiring as to whether she had yet acquired a new "beau," and buying her a ring ("Don't worry, I paid for it."). His fondness for her grows, and he begins to envision a life with Ed, a life not punctuated with visits to prison but one in which she saves him from the drift of his current life. Ed represents fulfillment for McDunnough, and while his earlier time in prison had been described in almost sentimental terms, his last stretch is spent longing for her love: "the joint is a lonely place after lockup and lights out, when the last of the cons has been swept away by the sandman. But I couldn't help thinking that a brighter future lay ahead—a future that was only eight to fourteen months away." McDunnough is a new man, reborn in prison through the love he now has for Ed. Background banjo picking, which had been regular throughout the introduction, turns noticeably into "Ode to Joy" (from Beethoven's Ninth Symphony), and Hi emerges from prison to propose to Ed at the police station, entering it "a free man."

McDunnough and wife start in earnest the process of procuring the American dream. Ed's father provides the young couple with a trailer, and McDunnough begins a respectable (if boring) job. "Mostways," he notes, "the job was a lot like prison, except Ed was waiting at the end of every day, and a paycheck at the end of every week." The couple is happy and make designs on raising a family. As McDunnough reflects:

> These were the happy days, the salad days, as they say, and Ed felt that having a critter was the next logical step. It was all she thought about. Her point was that there was too much love and beauty for just the two of us, and every day we kept a child out of the world was a day he might later regret having missed.

So Hi and Ed set out to have themselves a "critter," working at it, in true biblical fashion, "on the days we calculated most likely to be fruitful,"[9] as well as "most other days, just to be sure." They devote themselves to the task as they would a mission, conscious of the transformation that they hope will occur. As Hi recalls, expressing his maturation from youth to adult (and symbolically from savage to civilized), "Ed rejoiced that my lawless years were behind me, and that our child-rearing years lay ahead."

But then, as McDunnough puts it, "the roof caved in"; Ed reveals to McDunnough that she is "barren,"[10] meaning unable to bear children but also reinforcing the notion of lost souls wandering in search of salvation. McDunnough, incredulous, wonders how "this woman, who looked as fertile as the Tennessee Valley, could not bear children."[11] But it was true—"the doctor explained that [Ed's] insides were a rocky place where my seed could find no purchase."[12] Both are devastated. The one thing on which they had both counted to make their lives complete was now being denied them. They try adoption, but McDunnough's criminal record renders that option impossible. Their lives lose meaning, and the joys that had sustained them as husband and wife seem to disappear. Notes McDunnough:

> Biology and the prejudices of others conspired to keep us childless. Our love for each other was stronger than ever. But I preminisced no return of the salad days. The *pizzazz* had gone out of our lives. Ed lost all interest in both criminal justice and housekeeping. Soon after, she tendered her badge. Even my job seemed as dry and bitter as a hot prairie wind.

One of the two elements that had kept his life as a free man different from his life in prison—his relationship with Ed—is threatened, and McDunnough, our Everyman, is in jeopardy of a fall. If seed (both his and those referred to in the allusion to the text from the Gospel of Matthew) represent salvation, then he is as barren as his wife. He finds himself backsliding, "driving by convenience stores that weren't on the way home."

"The Answer to All Our Prayers":
The Desire for Salvation

Deliverance arrives when "the biggest news . . . hit the state since they built the Hoover Dam"—the birth of the Arizona "quints." Five boys (Harry, Barry, Larry, Garry, and Nathan Jr.) are born to Nathan and Florence Arizona. Arizona Sr. (played by Trey Wilson) is "the owner of the largest chain of unpainted furniture and bathroom fixtures outlets throughout the Southwest," a huckster whose stores ("Unpainted Arizona") and face are so omnipresent that they defy the need for explanation. As the narrator McDunnough notes when he is about to identify Arizona, "well, hell, you know who he is." We *don't* know who he is, but with a motto ("or my name ain't Nathan Arizona") reminiscent of the declaration of the divine identity throughout the Hebrew Scriptures ("I am the Lord"),[13] we will come to. By the end of the film, it will be plausible to understand Arizona as the representative of a deity figure in this morality play.[14]

The Arizona "quints" present McDunnough and Ed with their opportunity for happiness and fulfillment, and they hatch a plan to kidnap one of them. They head out to execute their plan, not for the monetary gain that might be had from any ransom Arizona might be willing to pay, but because they figure that "it was unfair that some should have so many while others should have so few."[15] McDunnough, obviously relating the tale after the conclusion of the event and reminding his listeners that "y'all who're without sin can cast the first stone,"[16] notes that "with the benefit of hindsight, maybe it wasn't such a hot idea, but at the time, Ed's little plan seemed like the solution to all our problems, and the answer to all our prayers." And nearly eleven minutes from the beginning of the story, as they set out to get themselves a baby, the opening titles finally roll.

"Sometimes It's a Hard World for Little Things": The Possibility of Deliverance

McDunnough's narration reminds us that he is looking back on the event after the fact, reflecting on his journey toward salvation. With the benefit of hindsight, he realizes that kidnapping the baby "wasn't such a hot idea," but at the time the baby represented a correction to his failed family planning, a filling of the void created by Ed's (and his) barrenness, and a restoration of his desires for salvation. It is therefore no surprise that his and his wife's attention focuses on the kidnapping of one of the Arizona babies. McDunnough, ever the well-meaning incompetent, fails at his first attempt to steal a child from the Arizona mansion, but with Ed's forceful direction ("You go right back up there and get me a toddler. I need a baby, Hi. They got more'n they can handle"), he returns to her with one of the infants. For a brief moment Ed wonders about the moral ramifications of their actions, but in the end she is comforted by her husband's lame philosophizing that "there's what's right and there's what's right, and never the twain shall meet." Satisfied, she bursts into tears, truly grateful and overwhelmed by the feelings that apparently accompany salvation. "I love him so much," she exclaims through her tears about a baby that is so unfamiliar to her yet represents so much.[17]

The symbolism of the "child-as-salvation" is reinforced throughout the film. Identified as an angel "straight from Heaven" by Dot, the wife of Hi's boss (and played by Frances McDormand), the child is constantly referred to as Nathan Junior, a strong indication that, although all are God's children (Harry, Barry, Larry, and Garry), only one is the son of God. This is reinforced by the translation of the very name "Nathan," a derivative of the Hebrew word for "gift." And just as the last name of the Christian savior was not "Christ," so too is the last name of the kidnapped infant not "Junior." It is not surprising that throughout the film Nathan Junior is constantly accompanied by a modern scripture, Dr. Spock's *Baby and Child Care*, a perfect association given the historic role that text has played in American child-raising. It makes sense that if one is to receive salvation, one must have the accompanying text (the Bible, as it were) to make sense of the gift. Thus, as McDunnough is upstairs selecting one of the infants to kidnap, Nathan (senior) and Florence Arizona are downstairs, where he is on the telephone conducting business and she—in middle-American conservative clothing, hair, and manner—is reading what appears to be the Bible but is actually the baby book. Indeed, wherever the child goes, so go (in McDunnough's words) "the instructions." Humanity may receive salvation, but it must also have the text to make it understandable.

Back at the homestead, Hi's transformation is seemingly complete. He cleanses the abode for the arrival of the savior, as it were; he hides what appears to be a pornographic magazine under the mattress, he puts "Home on the Range" on the children's record player, and he sets up his wife and new son for a family photo. Ed, apparently either unsatisfied with her husband's transformation or recognizing the irony of starting a new life of decency through the criminal act of kidnapping, asks Hi for assurances that everything will be "decent and normal from here on out." The resulting family photo reveals an anxious look on McDunnough's face, presaging trouble ahead.

The trouble is represented by two of McDunnough's former jailmates, Gale and Evelle Snopes (played by John Goodman and William Forsythe, respectively).[18] The brothers emerge from the mud after their escape from prison during a rainstorm, and in one shot project an image reminiscent of their Edenic snake role model at the same time that it acknowledges (but subverts) the birth of the biblical twins Jacob and Esau.[19] Once out of the muck, they both emit a primal scream similar to the one voiced by Florence Arizona when she realized that one of her children was missing. After cleaning themselves up (and stealing a getaway car), the brothers make their way to the McDunnough trailer only hours after Hi and Ed have returned from a night of kidnapping. Gale notices the infant and comments that McDunnough has "been up to the devil's bidnis"—suggesting sexual relations, but also unknowingly referring to the gravity of the crime of "soul stealing" that has been committed in order to attain salvation. When Ed indicates that, as criminals, the Snopes brothers are not welcome in the home, Gale begins to tempt Hi by questioning his masculinity ("Who wears the pants around here, H.I.?") and his authority in the marriage ("Gotcha on a awful short leash, don't she, H.I.?"). McDunnough responds with a sly yet knowing wink.

Of course, Hi cannot withhold the truth from his wife. Later in their bedroom, Ed notes that Gale and Evelle are fugitives and asks Hi how they are "gonna start a new life with them around?" Hi reveals his good nature (as well as implied knowledge of the Bible) by replying that "you gotta have a little charity. Ya know, in Arab lands they'd set out a plate."[20] Ed's fears will later be realized when Gale and Evelle reveal their real reason for arriving: to invite Hi to join them on a crime spree "across the entire Southwest proper."[21]

"It's a Crazy World." "Someone Ought to Sell Tickets": Temptation and the Fall of Man

And yet, this temptation offered by Gale and Evelle is trifling compared to the evil awaiting McDunnough. The night Gale and Evelle arrive, Hi dreams of "the lone biker of the apocalypse."[22] "He was horrible," notes McDunnough:

a man with all the power of hell at his command. He could turn the day into night, and laid to waste everything in his path. He was especially hard on the little things, the helpless and the gentle creatures. He left a scorched earth in his wake, befouling even the sweet desert breeze that whipped across his brow.

"I didn't know if he was a dream or vision," reflects McDunnough after the fact, "but I feared that I myself had unleashed him, for he was The Fury That Would Be as soon as Florence Arizona found her little Nathan gone."[23]

"The Fury That Would Be" arrives with a screaming Florence Arizona, which serves as both the conclusion to Hi's nightmare and the beginning of the reality of the kidnapping. McDunnough awakens to find his wife holding Nathan Junior, gently singing a song to quiet the infant.[24] "He all right?" asks Hi, to which Ed responds—reinforcing the link between the child and Hi—"He was just having a nightmare." "Sometimes it's a hard world for little things," reflects Hi.

If Hi is one of the little things, his reflection turns out to be true. After threatening to evict the Snopes brothers and spending the afternoon with his boss's family (an event that ends with the boss inviting Hi into the world of wife swapping and Hi punching his boss in the face), Hi resorts to his life of crime, holding up a convenience store clerk for "Huggies and whatever cash you got." After a long chase involving two gun-toting convenience store clerks, a squadron of trigger-happy police officers, and a pack of dogs, Hi is picked up by Ed and Nathan. "I'm not gonna live this way, Hi," Ed yells as they make their getaway. "It just ain't family life!" "Well . . . it ain't Ozzie and Harriet," replies Hi.

On their return home, after Ed has gone to sleep, Gale and Evelle offer Hi a stake in their crime-spree plan, inspired in part by information collected in prison from "one of Dick Nixon's undersecretaries of agriculture,"[25] and in part by the audacity of the Arizona baby kidnapping, which they have not yet traced back to Hi and Ed. Hi demurs, but Gale notes that "stayin' here, y'ain't doin' [Ed] any good. And y'ain't being true to your own nature."

Tempted, that night Hi writes a farewell letter to Ed:

My dearest Edwinna,

Tonight as you and Nathan slumber, my heart is filled with anguish. I hope that you will both understand, and forgive me for what I have decided I must do. By the time you read this, I will be gone. I will never be the man that you want me to be, the husband and father that you and Nathan deserve. Maybe it's my upbringing; maybe it's just that my genes got screwed up—I don't know. But the events of the last day have showed, amply, that I don't have the strength of character to raise up a family in the manner befitting a responsible adult. I say all this to my shame. I will love you always, truly and deeply. But I fear that if I stay I would only bring bad trouble on the heads of you and Nathan Jr. I feel the thunder gathering even now; if I leave, hopefully it will leave with me. I cannot tarry. Better I should go, send you money, and let you curse my name. Your loving, Herbert.

Hi falls asleep writing the note, unaware of the real adventure that lies ahead.

"My Friends Call Me Lenny, Only I Ain't Got No Friends": The Presence of Evil

As Hi writes his note to Ed preparing her for his departure, the "lone biker of the apocalypse" grows closer to his encounter with our Everyman. He has been tracking Hi, Gale, and Evelle since he materialized out of Hi's nightmare, and in a scene that confirms this character's role as Evil while it strengthens the divinity of Nathan Sr., we have one of our most intriguing biblical references.

Hi's "lone biker of the apocalypse," Leonard Smalls[26]—a constant presence of dirt, sweat, smoke, and flame—barges into Arizona's office and announces "You got flies." "I doubt it," responds

Arizona. "This place is climate controlled. All the windows are sealed. Who the hell are you?" Smalls indicates that he is there to conduct business; he's a manhunter, a tracker, and (introducing the notion of satanic parallelism) "part hounddog." When he suggests that he does "hunt babies on occasion," Arizona takes umbrage and notes that he already has a flock of law enforcement officials looking for his baby. "Cop won't find your boy," replies Smalls. "Cop couldn't find his butt if it had a bell on it. Wanna find an outlaw, call an outlaw. Wanna find a Dunkin Donuts, call a cop." The two discuss terms for the baby's return, and when Arizona indicates that there is a twenty-five thousand dollar reward posted for the return of the baby, Smalls suggests that the fee is determined by the market, not by Arizona. In a second vaguely satanic reference, Smalls indicates that "as a pup," he had been sold on the black market for thirty thousand dollars, "and that was 1954 dollars." "For fifty grand," Smalls announces, "I'll track him, find him, and"—leaping up to snag a fly in midair just in front of Arizona's face—"I'll kick their butts. No extra charge." The scene comes to a close as Arizona rejects Smalls's offer: "I think you're an evil man. I think this is nothin' but a goddam screw job. I think it's a shakedown." And as Arizona threatens to call the police, Smalls disappears in a cloud of his own cigar smoke.

The scene is clearly necessary for the development of the plot; by bringing together Smalls and Arizona, all of the characters continue to converge to the movie's climax. However, the role of the fly at the beginning and end of the scene is indeed an odd bit of framing but also necessary in the development of Smalls as the representation of evil. Identified as the "lone biker of the apocalypse" by McDunnough, "an evil man" by Arizona, and, in the film's climax scene, a "warthog from Hell" by Ed, Smalls's relationship to the flies cements his identity within the morality play format; one of the many names given to Satan in the Hebrew Scriptures is Ba'al ze'vuv (often pronounced Beelzebub), which translates from the Hebrew as "lord of the flies."

"The First Day of the Rest of Your Life":
The Confrontation between Everyman and Evil

The unleashing of evil begins to take its toll. Hi is awakened the next morning by Gale and Evelle, rousing him to his life of crime and presciently noting that "today is the first day of the rest of your life." It will be, indeed. As Hi prepares to leave with the Snopes brothers, his boss (with black eye and neck brace) arrives and announces that he knows where the new McDunnough baby has come from. If Hi does not turn the child over when Dot (the boss's wife) returns for the child, he will report Hi and Ed to the authorities.

Hi returns to his trailer to find Gale and Evelle holding Nathan Junior, intent on kidnapping the child themselves. A fight ensues—Hi is, after all, fighting to protect his own salvation—with the brothers overpowering Hi. They leave him tied up in his own trailer, only to return moments later to retrieve that most important document that must accompany the baby—Dr. Spock's *Baby and Child Care.* As Gale and Evelle set out to rob a bank with their new partner, Hi lets out a wail similar to that let out by Florence Arizona when she discovered her Nathan Junior missing or when the Snopes brothers emerged from prison.

Upon Ed's return (she had been out running errands), Hi describes what has happened and prepares himself to retrieve Nathan Junior from the Snopes brothers, who were "just in it for the score." Hi, on the other hand, realizes the value of what he has lost and vows that he is "a changed man." Reassuring Ed, he notes "you were right and I was wrong. We got a family here and I'm gonna start acting responsibly."

Meanwhile, as Gale and Evelle drive toward their crime target, they begin to realize the value of that which they have purloined. In the car, Evelle notes that the baby smiled at him (which, given the salvationary role of the infant, is vaguely reminiscent of the Christmas carol in which the baby Jesus smiles at the little drummer boy), and when they return after inadvertently leaving the child at a convenience store they have robbed for some baby food, diapers, and balloons (and giving the now requisite scream), they vow to "never give him up." Notes Gale, reinforcing the commodified salvationary importance of the infant: "He's our little Gale Jr. now." Observed one reviewer, "Junior transforms all those in whose care he is placed."[27]

As all of the characters race toward the film's climax, Hi and Ed finally realize what it is that they have actually done, and the light of salvation through self-knowledge finally shines through. As they race to catch up with Gale and Evelle, Hi tries to console Ed, but Ed reflects on their shared journey: "I don't care about myself anymore," she notes, "I don't care about us anymore. I just want Nathan Junior back safe." She suggests that even if they are successful at retrieving the child, she is unsure she wants to continue being married to Hi. "We don't deserve Nathan Jr. Any more'n those jailbirds do. And if I'm as selfish and irresponsible as you"—(Hi interrupts: "You ain't *that* bad, honey.") "If I'm as bad as you, what good're we to each other? You'n me's just a fool's paradise." Unlike Hi's boss and his wife, and unlike Gale and Evelle, Ed finally realizes that she really has been barren and that salvation means personal transformation and does not come from something attained from without, such as the long hoped-for child.

Hi and Ed catch up with Gale and Evelle, but not before the two brothers have robbed the bank and again left the baby behind. Hi and Ed demand to know where the child is, and as they leave to get him (but again, *not* before retrieving Dr. Spock's *Baby and Child Care* from the brothers' getaway car), Gale can be heard yelling "let us come with you. He's our baby, too!"

As they approach the bank to retrieve the child, Hi and Ed see ahead of them the fireball marking the approach of Smalls and the appearance of true evil. "What is he?" asks Ed, and for the first time, Hi realizes that this vision he had in a nightmare is now real: "D'you see him, too?" he responds. Smalls has beaten them to the child, and Nathan Junior is now perched—in his carseat—firmly between the handlebars of Smalls's motorcycle as he prepares to square off with Hi. Prepared to meet her own doom, Ed approaches Smalls, demanding that he give her the baby. As Smalls prepares to throw a knife at Ed, Hi fires his own handgun (which, as far as we know, is the first time it has been loaded in his entire life of crime) and hits the knives just as Ed takes the child. A chase and fight ensue in which Hi exposes Smalls's Woody Woodpecker tattoo that they share—suggesting that the evil that is Smalls may actually be part (or a reflection) of McDunnough. Finally, as Smalls throttles him, Hi is able to grab the pin out of one of the many hand grenades that hang from Small's vest. Unable to stop the impending explosion, Smalls looks innocently at Hi. "I'm sorry," Hi whispers from across the parking lot, as Smalls explodes.

With evil now destroyed, Hi and Ed do the only thing left they can do—return Nathan Junior to his rightful home. Notes Jeffrey Mahan, "moral and physical restoration are comedy's proper ending,"[28] and this film ends where it began—not before the eleven-minute prologue, but at the Arizona household, where Hi and Ed began their journey toward salvation. Baby and (burnt) *Baby and*

Child Care back where they belong, the McDunnoughs are sharing one last glimpse of the child when they are discovered by Arizona Senior. When Arizona demands an explanation, Hi notes that "in a re-ward situation, they usually say no questions asked." Arizona, fulfilling his role as symbolic deity, acknowledges the financial reward but indicates a preference for issuing a store credit to the McDunnoughs instead (suggesting delayed and intangible—rather than immediate and tangible—rewards) and is thrilled when Ed admits that they didn't bring the child back for the money, making it a truly altruistic act. "*You* took him, didn't you?" remarks Arizona, "wasn't that biker a'tall." Hi and Ed confess their sin, each trying to shield the other from blame. "Just tell me," asks Arizona, "why you did it." "We can't have one of our own," admits Ed. Arizona encourages the couple to keep trying (to have faith?) and suggests that even if they remain unsuccessful, the inability to have a child is not the end of the world. "You still got each other," he notes. When Hi suggests that he and Ed have decided to split up, Arizona encourages them to stay together. "I don't know much but I do know human bein's. You brought back my boy so you must have your good points too." He suggests that they sleep on it before making any decisions. Arizona suggests that Hi and Ed can "go out the way you came in," a reference to their sneaking into his house through the window but also a deceptive admonition that people may leave the world in the same state in which they entered it, in need of perfection.[29]

At the end of this "first day" of the rest of his life, Hi has a dream of the future that awaits him. He sees Gale and Evelle return to prison through the hole from which they had emerged. He sees Nathan Junior receiving a Christmas present "from a kindly couple who preferred to remain unknown" who, watching Nathan become a young man, take pride "in his accomplishments as if he were our own." Finally, he dreams of his own future with Ed. He sees "an old couple bein' visited by their children—and all their grandchildren too." He notes that "the old couple wasn't screwed up, and neither were their kids, or their grandkids." He ponders whether this is to be reality or was he "fleein' reality, like I know I'm liable to do?" "It *seemed* real," he notes. "It *seemed* like us." Maybe it was them, he concludes, if not now, and not here, then in "a land, not *too* far away, where all parents are strong and wise and capable, and all children are happy and beloved . . . I dunno," he concludes, "maybe it was Utah."[30]

"Was It All Wishful Thinking?"
Reading Religion from Film

It is entirely possible that none of the religious analysis of *Raising Arizona* has any relation to reality. Many critics suggested the film was simply a reflection of the more important secular themes of the 1980s—"having babies and taking hostages," noted *Washington Post* reviewer Rita Kempley.[31] And to be sure, the film does critically examine the frantic desire to grab on to the American dream and its manifestations in parenthood, homeownership, and, as Hi notes wryly, all things "Ozzie and Harriet." But just as many, if not more, reviewers were highly critical of this film. As Janet Maslin wrote in the *New York Times*: "To the extent that films are about ideas, *Raising Arizona* isn't about anything, and it tells its story in a spirit of technical accomplishment rather than in the interests of narrative momentum."[32] Sheila Benson wondered how the film could "move so fast, be so loud and remain so relentlessly boring at the same time."[33] And the high priest of popular movie criticism, Roger Ebert, gave the movie one and one-half stars, exclaiming that it was "all over the map."[34]

Joel Martin, in the introduction to a collection of essays on religion and film, notes that, at times, "little is to be gained by examining every film in relation to religion,"[35] and there is always a risk of reading too much into a film. Reflecting on *Raising Arizona* and *Blood Simple* (Joel and Ethan Coen's first major release), Bruce Bawer has suggested that, on the one hand, "the films of the Coen brothers, for all their absurdity, nevertheless reflect an acute and pained awareness of the evil of which human beings are capable." However, at the same time, he concludes that "to go on too long about such matters would be to suggest that the film is more serious than it is."[36] The film is, after all, a comedy, and relies more on humor than on morality to deliver its message.

How, then, should we understand all of the religious parallels in this film, from the biblical language to the morality play structure, from the off-hand references to Satan to the symbolism of salvation?

In his 1988 book *Cultural Literacy*, E. D. Hirsch Jr. argued that American youth were ill-prepared for the world of business (and, one can assume, other endeavors) because they did not share a core body of knowledge that enabled them to be "culturally literate" and therefore able to communicate effectively and efficiently with others. He defined cultural literacy as "the network of information that

all competent readers possess." He noted that culturally literate people were those who could communicate effectively in the idiom of
society:

> It is the background information, stored in their minds, that enables
> them to take up a newspaper and read it with an adequate level of com-
> prehension, getting the point, grasping the implications, relating what
> they read to the unstated context which alone gives meaning to what
> they read.[37]

He suggested that one need not possess an expert's knowledge of
everything to be a "competent reader"—as long as one has some
sense of the basic "givens" in our society, one will generally understand what is being communicated.[38]

Though his book and the supplements that followed were the subject of considerable debate and criticism, there is little doubt that
cultural products in our society, including the variety of artistic
media, often presume a basic level of competence on the part of
the viewer in order to communicate deeper levels of nuance and
symbolism. We might even argue that there are a variety of different
modes of communication with which one must be, at a minimum,
conversational in order to be considered culturally literate. This is
no less true of religion, and, in the Western world, this has meant
being cognizant of the basic stories, symbols, and structures of Judaism and Christianity, even if one is not traditionally educated in
them.[39]

But if this is so, and one accepts the premise that a film with such
demonstrably religious parallels and symbolism as *Raising Arizona*
has been overlooked for its religious content and structure (and not
simply dismissed for it), then there are at least two factors that might
explain why several reviewers, and uncounted viewers, missed much
(if not all) of the religious nuance in this film. First, American culture has become increasingly religiously diverse, most notably since
the mid-1960s, when changes to citizenship laws expanded immigration, particularly from Asia.[40] As a result, religions other than Judaism and Christianity have grown in raw numbers in the population
and subsequently have asserted themselves into the public consciousness, making traditionally Western symbolism less dominant.
Examples of this phenomenon can be found in many places, including on bookstore shelves which contain works on Yoga, Tantra, and
other forms of non-Western religiosity. Second, and in conjunction

with this diversification of American religious culture, there has been a marked trend away from institutional forms of religiosity.[41] According to Wade Clark Roof, "baby boomers"—particularly those with a high level of exposure to the major events of the late 1960s—are marked by their willingness to move beyond institutional religions. They have become, to use the title of his work, a "generation of seekers."[42] Phillip Hammond argues that this generation more than any before it has felt released of any denominational or institutional loyalties and obligations, making its members less and less likely to end their lives with the religious affiliation with which they began them.[43] Increasing numbers of this generation, suspicious of social institutions such as government (possibly as a result of the criticism surrounding American involvement in the Vietnam War or the general disappointment accompanying the Watergate scandal) and religion (as embodying much of the "establishment" mentality of their parents and the ethos of the 1950s),[44] have felt a greater freedom to pursue individual—rather than communal—forms of spiritual identification and have therefore felt free to explore among the many religious options in American culture, including nontraditional and seemingly secular alternatives.[45] As a result, the children of this generation of seekers, the so-called Generation X, have had even less grounding in the traditional forms of institutional religion than their parents. While the parents may have been dragged to church as children and rebelled against it as young adults, they still are likely to have been exposed to the stories, symbols, and structures present in traditional Western religions. Their own children, less likely to have been dragged to church by "baby boomer" parents who have now become "seekers," are therefore also less likely to have the basic foundation of Western religious culture. Their religiosity, as evident in the preferred self-identification as "spiritual" (as opposed to "religious"), is marked by an experiential, noninstitutional, popular cultural quality that often lacks clear traditional referents.[46] Understanding of, and fluency in, religious elements—elements that were once taken for granted as fundamental in Western cultural literacy—has been lost as fewer Americans are exposed to those elements once considered basic.

Did the Coen brothers consciously construct their film to reflect religious symbolism and structure? Probably not. Having been raised in an Orthodox Jewish home, it is likely that they were exposed to Western religious imagery, at least that found in the Hebrew Scriptures.[47] More significantly, the two brothers were familiar with a different canon: the films and television shows that have been such a large part of culture formation in contemporary American society. "In fact," notes biographer Josh Levine, "it might well be that television-watching was the biggest influence of all" on the Coens.[48] These programs provided the Coens, and many of their generation and since, with the fundamental tools to understand and interpret their surroundings. They were, in the words of American religious historian Catherine Albanese, "mass culture brokers,"[49] and as such they provided for their viewers what in previous generations had been provided by other (possibly more traditional) means. Thus, it is entirely possible that the Coen brothers were not at all intending to suffuse their film with religious symbolism or to construct it in the form of a morality play. They were just using materials from a culture that retained these images and narrative structures as remnants from a not-so-distant past in which more people were exposed to formal religious training in traditional religious environments.

But even if the Coen brothers did not realize they were following a primarily Christian model of storytelling or making use of religious references from both the Hebrew and the Christian Scriptures, it is still revealing that these images are there to be found and just as revealing that they are so easily overlooked by so many. Hirsch's theory argues that cultures develop a shorthand symbol system for communicating complex ideas. While his concern was that fewer American students were being taught how to use that system to communicate effectively in the idiom of the general culture, it seems that with changes in the role and status of institutional religion in America this is not only a matter of concern over what constitutes cultural literacy. In contemporary America, with more and more people moving further and further from traditional religion as their source of meaning construction and maintenance, larger and larger segments of the population will continue to use that symbolic cultural shorthand as part of their mode of communication but will be unable to interpret its meaning or place it in context. Fewer and fewer people will be religiously literate enough to understand, and half of the stories' meanings will be left on the proverbial cutting-room floor as references like those found in movies like *Raising Arizona* become remnants of the culture's religious identity. And while the fear that fewer people will appreciate the nuance of a comedy like *Raising Arizona* seems important, it should give us pause when we consider that the same symbols, images, and narrative structures function throughout the arts in the West. Might it be that fewer people will be religiously literate enough to understand the more sublime, intellectual, or abstract arts if they cannot even see religion's imprint in a straightforward comedy like *Raising Arizona*? As Hi would say, that'd be a damn shame.

Notes

1. The video cassette adds a subtitle: "A Comedy beyond Belief."

2. Comedies have gotten little attention in scholarly writing on religion and film. See Robert Jewett, *St. Paul Returns to the Movies: Triumph Over Shame* (Grand Rapids, Mich.: Eerdmans, 1998); Clive Marsh and Gaye Ortiz, eds., *Explorations in Theology and Film* (Malden, Mass.: Blackwell, 1997); Margaret R. Miles, *Seeing and Believing: Religion and Values in the Movies* (Boston: Beacon Press, 1996); Joel W. Martin and Conrad Ostwalt Jr., eds., *Screening the Sacred: Religion, Myth, and Ideology in Popular American Film* (Boulder, Colo.: Westview Press, 1995); Robert Jewett, *St. Paul at the Movies: The Apostle's Dialogue with Modern Culture* (Louisville, Ky.: Westminster John Knox Press, 1993); and John R. May and Michael Bird, eds., *Religion in Film* (Knoxville: The University of Tennessee Press, 1982). The online *Journal of Religion and Film*, <http://www.unomaha.edu/~wwwjrf/>) has provided a forum for the discussion of religion in comic as well as dramatic films but as of this writing has not published an article on *Raising Arizona.*

3. David Bevington defines the morality play as "the dramatization of a spiritual crisis in the life of a representative mankind figure in which his spiritual struggle is portrayed as a conflict between personified abstractions representing good and evil." He suggests that the most common plot involves "a soul-struggle in which the mankind hero succumbs to vice but is finally restored to grace." See David Bevington, *Medieval Drama* (Boston: Houghton Mifflin, 1975), 792.

4. Ibid.

5. Quoted in Robert Jewett and John Shelton Lawrence, *The American Monomyth* (Garden City, N.Y.: Anchor Press, 1977), 3.

6. The direct quotations in this essay have been taken from the film version. However, I consulted the published screenplay for confirmation and use of dialect. See Joel Coen and Ethan Coen, *Raising Arizona: The Screenplay* (New York: St. Martin's Press, 1988).

7. Roger Ebert, film critic for the *Chicago Sun-Times*, seemed to miss the point when he noted that "everyone in *Raising Arizona* talks funny." "*Raising Arizona*," *Chicago Sun-Times*, 20 March 1987.

8. The dialogue at one of McDunnough's parole hearings:

CHAIRMAN: They got a name for people like you, Hi. That name is called recidivism.
SECOND MAN: Ree-peat O-fender.
CHAIRMAN: Not a pretty name, is it, Hi?
HI: No, sir, it sure ain't. That's one bonehead name. But that ain't me anymore.
CHAIRMAN: You're not just telling us what we wanna hear?
HI: No sir, no way.
SECOND MAN: 'Cause we just want to hear the truth.

HI: Well, then I guess I *am* telling you what you wanna hear.
CHAIRMAN: Boy, didn't we just tell you not to do that?
HI: Yessir.
CHAIRMAN: Okay, then.

9. "And God blessed them, and God said unto them, 'Be fruitful, and multiply'" (Gen. 1:28). According to BibleontheWeb.com, the word *fruitful* is repeated thirty-three times in the King James translation of the Hebrew Scriptures. For the purposes of this essay, all biblical references are from the King James Version of the Christian Bible.

10. "And Isaac intreated the Lord for his wife, because she was barren" (Gen. 25:21). According to BibleontheWeb.com, the word *barren* is repeated nineteen times in the King James translation of the Hebrew Scriptures.

11. See Gen. 41:47.

12. "Some [seeds] fell upon stony places, where they had not much earth: and forthwith they sprung up, because they had no deepness of earth: And when the sun was up, they were scorched; and because they had no root, they withered away" (Matt. 13:5–6). The reference here is to the gospel, making the use of the "seed" in the film a reference to salvation as well as insemination.

13. According to BibleontheWeb.com, the phrase "I am the Lord" is repeated 163 times in the King James translation of the Hebrew Scriptures.

14. As it turns out, Arizona's name isn't Arizona—we later learn that he has changed it from Huffhines, identifying the character's desire to seem more American while paralleling the accounting of the names of God in Exod. 6:2–3. Interestingly, there is a town named Florence, Arizona, but there is no Nathan, Arizona.

15. "For I mean not that other men be eased, and ye burdened: But by an equality, that now at this time your abundance may be a supply for their want, that their abundance also may be a supply for your want: that there may be equality" (2 Cor. 8:13–14).

16. "So when they continued asking him, he lifted up himself, and said unto them, He that is without sin among you, let him first cast a stone at her" (John 8:7).

17. Ed is clearly exhibiting what in the Christian Scriptures was referred to in Greek as *agape*, which the *Oxford English Dictionary* defines as "Christian love (of God or Christ or fellow Christian"), as opposed to erotic or sexual love. This type of love is commonly expressed within both the Hebrew and Christian Scriptures and is even commanded on a number of occasions: "ye shall hearken diligently unto my commandments which I command you this day, to love the LORD your God, and to serve him with all your heart and with all your soul" (Deut. 11:13; compare Matt. 22:37, Mark 12:30, Luke 10:27).

18. One movie critic suggests that the last name is "a jokey reminder of Faulkner's Yoknapatawpha County." See Vincent Camby, "*Raising Arizona*: Coen Brothers Comedy," *New York Times*, 11 March 1987, C24.

19. In a twist on the biblical account, the more Esau-like Gale pulls Evelle from the muddy hole by his heel. See Gen. 25:25–27.

20. See the story of Abraham and the three strangers (Gen. 18:2–5).

21. The title of this essay, which Gale uses to introduce his crime-spree offer to Hi, is therefore an ironic twist of a portion of the Sermon on the Mount: "Neither do men light a candle, and put it under a bushel, but on a candlestick; and it giveth light unto all that are in the house. Let your light so shine before men, that they

may see your good works, and glorify your Father which is in heaven" (Matt. 5:15–16).

22. The reference is an allusion to the four horsemen of the apocalypse. See Rev. 6:2–8.

23. Identifying this character as "The Fury That Would Be" reinforces the close connection between him and Hi—he becomes not only a vision of evil that Hi has created in his dream but an instrument of God similar to other forces in biblical literature (including the Babylonians and the Persians). The "fury" is used in the Hebrew Scriptures to characterize God's anger toward his wayward people (see Jer. 36:7).

24. The song is the traditional bluegrass ballad "Down in the Willow Garden." Ed is singing in the background:

> My father sits at his cabin door, wiping his tear dimmed eyes,
> For his only son soon shall walk to yonder scaffold high.
> My race is run beneath the sun, the scaffold now waits for me,
> For I did murder that dear little girl whose name was Rose Connelly.

25. A hierarchy of evil is reinforced by Gale's admission that "ordinarily we don't associate with that class of person," suggesting that even thieves have standards.

26. One scholar notes the similarities between *Raising Arizona* and John Steinbeck's *Of Mice and Men*, using this character's name of Leonard Smalls as a particular point of intersection. See Rodney Hill, "Small Things Considered: *Raising Arizona* and *Of Mice and Men*," *Post Script* 8, no. 3 (Summer 1989): 18–27.

27. Jeffrey H. Mahan, "*Raising Arizona*," *The Christian Century* 104, 1 July 1987, 598.

28. Ibid.

29. God says to Adam and Eve after they have eaten the forbidden fruit: " 'for dust thou art, and unto dust shalt thou return' " (Gen. 3:19).

30. This reference to Utah and numerous children—a seemingly off-hand reference to Mormonism—reinforces the religious aspect of *Raising Arizona*; indeed, Mormonism was, according to Leo Tolstoy, "*the* American religion." See Klaus J. Hansen, *Quest for Empire: The Political Kingdom of God and the Council of Fifty in Mormon History* (East Lansing: Michigan State University Press, 1967), 25.

31. Rita Kempley, "*Raising Arizona*," *Washington Post*, 20 March 1987, 29.

32. Janet Maslin, "What Is a New Director?" *New York Times*, 29 March 1987, sec. 2, p. 17.

33. Sheila Benson, "Two Unlikely Love Affairs; *Raising Arizona*: Farcing Around with Parenthood," *Los Angeles Times*, 20 March 1987, sec. 6, p. 1.

34. Ebert, "*Raising Arizona*."

35. Martin, "Introduction: Seeing the Sacred on the Screen," in Martin and Ostwalt, eds., *Screening the Sacred*, 4.

36. Bruce Bawer, *The Screenplay's the Thing: Movie Criticism, 1986–1990* (Hamden, Conn.: Archon Books, 1992), 66.

37. E. D. Hirsch Jr., *Cultural Literacy: What Every American Needs to Know*, updated and expanded (New York: Vintage Books, 1988), 2.

38. He provides a list of "What Literate Americans Know"—sixty-three pages of terms such as "Hank Aaron," "Abandon hope, all ye who enter here," "abbreviation," and "Aberdeen" (the first four from the list). See ibid., 152–215.

39. This is not to suggest that knowledge of non-Western religious traditions is unimportant or that it is not increasingly important, but it is significantly less important when one compares it to the impact Judaism and Christianity have had on cultural production in the United States.

40. See Gordon J. Melton, "Another Look at New Religions," *Annals of the American Academy of Political and Social Science* 527 (May 1993), 97–112.

41. See Robert Wuthnow, *After Heaven: Spirituality in America since the 1950s* (Berkeley: University of California Press, 1998).

42. Wade Clark Roof, *A Generation of Seekers* (San Francisco, Calif.: Harper SanFrancisco, 1993). "Exposure" is defined by participation in protests, use of marijuana, and attendance at rock concerts.

43. Phillip E. Hammond, *Religion and Personal Autonomy: The Third Disestablishment in America* (Columbia: University of South Carolina Press, 1992).

44. See Wuthnow, *After Heaven*, particularly 19–51.

45. For examples of how nontraditional and seemingly secular pursuits come to fill the place of traditional religious practice, see Eric Michael Mazur and Kate McCarthy, eds., *God in the Details: American Religion in Popular Culture* (New York: Routledge, 2001).

46. See Tom Beaudoin, *Virtual Faith: The Irreverent Spiritual Quest of Generation X* (San Francisco, Calif.: Jossey-Bass, 1998).

47. Ronald Bergan, *The Coen Brothers* (New York: Thunder's Mouth Press, 2000), 41–42.

48. Josh Levine, *The Coen Brothers: The Story of Two American Filmmakers* (Toronto: ECW Press, 2000), 5.

49. Catherine L. Albanese, "Religion and Popular Culture: An Introductory Essay," *Journal of the American Academy of Religion* 59, no. 4 (Fall 1996): 740.

The Art of Idolatry:
Violent Expressions of the Spiritual in Contemporary Performance Art

Dawn Perlmutter
Cheyney University of Pennsylvania

THE traditional Western conception of religious art includes paintings, sculpture, and prints of beautiful Madonnas, biblical scenes, and devotional images. In the twenty-first century manifestations of the spiritual in art have significantly changed. Artists' materials no longer consist of just paint and clay but incorporate every available substance including bodily fluids. Artworks encompass everything from religious paintings done in the artist's own blood to installations creating entire sacred spaces, performance art where sacrificial rituals are enacted, body mutilations as an aesthetic form of mortification, and earthworks designed to inspire nature worship.

Ironically, many of the contemporary forms of sacred art embody religious prohibitions on image worship found throughout biblical literature. Sometimes these are intentional acts of blasphemy to provoke controversy; more often they are authentic attempts by artists to reclaim the spiritual in their lives. These aesthetic expressions have been assimilated into popular culture in the current popularity of tattooing, piercing, branding, and body modifications. These unconventional forms of the sacred manifested in art and adopted into popular culture have provoked censorship on many levels of society. Essentially, they challenge the fundamental values and religious monotheism of Western culture.

Performance Art and Performance Artists

A phenomenon in contemporary art is taking place in which highly ritualized and often violent actions by visual artists are classi-

fied under the aesthetic genre of performance art. For most of us who are unfamiliar with the avant-garde art world, performance art signifies the theater arts such as ballet, modern dance, musicals, dramas, etc., and are performed by actors and dancers. Although it entails many of the characteristics of theater arts, performance art evolved specifically in the context of visual art and from an entirely different historical position. The origins of contemporary performance art extend back to the Italian Futurist artists of the early 1900s when Filippo Marinetti, a member of this group, performed an evening of special events in Trieste, Italy in 1910. Six years later this was followed by a series of performances by the Dadaists in Zurich. Most of the events were nihilistic in character and reflected the horror of the recent war in Europe. Many of the same concerns and actions reemerged in the late fifties and were referred to as Live-Action, Painters Events, Body Art, and Happenings. Many of the Happenings were multimedia events and incorporated live sound, projected images, and body movement.[1] In the late sixties and early seventies, performance art became accepted as a medium of artistic expression in its own right, incorporating traditional forms of painting and sculpture, theater, photography, music, dance, technology, politics, and popular culture. At the turn of the twenty-first century, there are many distinct varieties of performance art, and although they elude specific categorization, there are environmental, media, technology, body, feminist, and ritual performance artists from every continent. The focus in this essay is on contemporary performance art that encompasses a variety of highly ritualized violent self-mutilations as expressions of the spiritual. Although this may seem like a very specialized genre, there are literally hundreds of artists whose artistic medium consists of the flesh and blood of their own body.

Performance artist Chris Burden did not paint or sculpt a crucifixion; in 1974 in a work titled "Trans-Fixed," he had himself crucified to a car. In the 1970s, Burden's art performances also included having himself shot with a gun, punctured, burned, and run over by a car. Burden's body became the ultimate sculptural material, the ultimate object. Artist Gina Pane does art performances that consist of self-inflicted cuts to her body, including her face. In 1971 she performed "Escalade non-anesthesie" in which she climbed a ladder that had blades attached to the steps. In 1972, in a performance titled "The Conditioning" (part 1 of "Auto-Portrait[s]"), she laid down on an iron bed with very few crossbars that had fifteen long candles burning underneath. In her book *Performance Art from Futur-*

ism to the Present, art historian Roselee Goldberg states that Pane "believed that ritualized pain had a purifying effect and that using blood, fire, milk and the re-creation of pain as the elements of her performances she succeeded in her own terms 'in making the public understand right off that my body is my artistic material.' "[2] In 1974 in a performance titled "Psyche," she knelt in front of a mirror, put on makeup, and proceeded to cut into her face with a razor blade. In 1975 in "Le corps pressenti," she made cuts between her toes with a razor blade so that the blood would create permanent stains on a plaster cast on which her feet were resting. In the exhibition catalogue *Out of Actions: Between Performance and the Object, 1949–1979*, curator Paul Schimmel referred to Pane's performances as "nonreligious sacraments."[3] In 1974 artist Petr Stembera performed an action titled "Narcissus #1" in which he stood gazing at a self-portrait placed on an altar surrounded by lit candles. Blood was drawn from his body with a hypodermic needle; Stembera then proceeded to mix the blood with his own urine, hair, and nail clippings, finally drinking the mixture in front of his altar. Kristine Stiles, in the catalogue *Out of Actions*, described Stembera's performance: "Such an action recalls shamanistic and voodoo practices for accumulating power, protecting against evil spirits, and generally guarding the soul."[4] These are just a few expressions of the spiritual manifested in self-mutilation as a form of performance art.

Beginning in the 1960s and culminating in the 1970s, there were several European artists who performed ritualized violent actions that focused on the body. The most famous of these was a circle of Viennese artists that included Hermann Nitsch, Gunter Brus, Otto Muehl, and Rudolph Schwartzkogler. These artists utilized several artistic mediums including painting, assemblage, drawing, photography, and collage, and created and participated in what was referred to as action-happenings. Brus and Muehl were more concerned with creating political statements through the use of photography and collage; however, their images also used religious symbolism, blood-drenched bodies, and violent mutilations. Hubert Klocker, curator of Collection Friedrichshof, Vienna, notes that "Nitsch and Schwartzkogler employ the magical gesture by assuming the role of the shaman or the priest. Brus, on the other hand, uses the body as a projection surface for the subconscious collective potential. It then turns into an expression of the sacrificial act."[5] However, their work was fundamentally different than the American Happenings and Fluxus movements in that it was based on the tradition of surrealism, which accounts for the overwhelming prevalence of blood and violence. Their work, which influenced many American artists in the nineties, became known as Viennese Actionism, and their interests included the cult of Dionysus, the rituals of the Catholic church, and the psychoanalytic theories of Sigmund Freud, Karl Jung, and Wilhelm Reich.[6]

Nitsch did a series of performances titled "Orgies-Mysteries-Theater" that frequently entailed the dismemberment of animals, large quantities of blood, and traditional religious symbolism. A 1974 performance titled "48th Action" at the Munich Modernes Theater involved the disembowelment of a slaughtered lamb whose entrails and blood were poured over a nude man, while the drained animal was strung up over his head. Art historian Goldberg describes Nitsch's performance in terms of ritual:

> Such activities sprang from Nitsch's belief that humankind's aggressive instincts had been repressed and muted through the media. Even the ritual of killing animals, so natural to primitive man, had been removed from modern-day experience. These ritualized acts were a means of releasing that repressed energy as well as an act of purification and redemption through suffering.[7]

Nitsch is still conducting his "Orgies-Mysteries-Theaters," although now they last as long as six days and are often the object of protest by animal rights activists.

The most controversial of these artists is Schwartzkogler, who participated in Nitsch's actions and created works that he referred to as "artistic nudes—similar to a wreckage" in which he performed self-administered mutilations. Schwartzkogler died violently on 20 June 1969, prompting several conflicting reports regarding the circumstances of his death. Wrote art critic Robert Hughes in a 1972 issue of *Time* magazine:

> Schwartzkogler seems to have deduced that what really counts is not the application of paint, but the removal of surplus flesh. So he proceeded, inch by inch, to amputate his own penis, while a photographer recorded the act as an art event. In 1972, the resulting prints were reverently exhibited in that biennial motor show of Western art, Documenta V at Kassel. Successive acts of self-amputation finally did Schwartzkogler in.[8]

Art historian Stiles claims that this is one of the notorious myths surrounding performance artists; the real cause of Schwartzkogler's death were the injuries he sustained from jumping out a window while obsessed with Yves Klein's photomontage "Leap into the Void," which falsely depicted Klein jumping from a second-story window. Stiles also notes that Schwartzkogler had begun experimenting that year with physical health regimes which he hoped would cleanse and purify his own body and mind.[9] In either account, Schwartzkogler's death was a violent act inspired by his immersion in a violent aesthetic and has the quality of a failed purification ritual. This incident inadvertently created an aesthetic mythology in which suicide is hailed as the ultimate performance art, the completed sacrifice.

Performance Art, Ritual, and Idolatry

Many body modifications in performance art parallel non-Western religious rituals of various cultures and eras. Kim Hewitt reports that in an act similar to the practice of autosacrifice by Aztec priests who drew their own blood as an offering, performance artist Michael Journiac "made a pudding with his own blood and offered it for consumption by his audience."[10] She also describes Australian artist Stelarc, who has suspended himself "in different environments by ropes attached to hooks driven through his flesh," and although these acts are reminiscent of the rituals of some Plains and Northwest Native American communities, "he claims that these works are only involved with transcending normal human parameters including pain."[11] Performance artist Fakir Musafar has made it quite clear that his intentions are to perform live demonstrations of religious rituals and practices. Influenced by *National Geographic* and *Compton's Picture Encyclopedia* at an early age, Fakir began a "systematic, personal exploration of virtually every body modification and ritual practice known to man."[12] A small sample of his performances include hanging by fleshhooks while performing an Indian O-Kee-Pa ceremony, penis stretching with weights while performing sexual negation rituals of the Sadhu of India, having one-pound weights attached to his chest with fishhooks (enacting mystical practices, also of the Sadhu), and corseting his waist (enacting an initiation ritual of the Ibitoe). Fakir has been performing rituals and body modifications for over forty years.

According to biblical literature, art performances as expressions of the spiritual constitute idolatry in form, content, and ideology.

Julien Ries, quoting other scholars of religion, notes that those who have addressed the problem of defining idolatry have usually anthropomorphized the idol, suggesting that idolatry is that which results when any such object that is the subject of any form of worship (structured or not). He then defines idolatry as "divine worship of beings who are not God in the eyes of those who have defined worship as idolatrous," noting that the word *idolatry* "has a negative and pejorative connotation because to the faithful of a monotheistic religion, attitudes, behaviors, and rites that should be strictly reserved for the true God are turned by the idolater toward false gods." He concludes, "idolatry is a fundamental religious disequilibrium due to two paradoxical facts: on the one hand a divine cultus, on the other a substitute for the divine that is not God."[13]

The biblical injunction against idolatry consists of three separate matters: the worship of idols, the worship of God with pagan rites, and the making of idols. Some of the biblical proscriptions include "idol worship conforming to the pagan rituals" (Exod. 20:5; Deut. 12:30); "bowing down" (Exod. 34:14); "offering a sacrifice to another god" (Exod. 22:19); and "paying homage to an idol" (Exod. 20:5). The Bible presents idolatry not merely as the worshiping of images but as the worshiping of anything, real or imaginary, other than God Himself. In the Bible, the religious and mythological values of the pagan world are not recognized, and the pagan claim that idolatry actually represents religious values is rejected.[14]

Initially, biblical prohibitions may not seem pertinent to contemporary performance art, but there should be no question of their current relevance. When performance artist Nitsch sacrifices animals as purification rituals he is committing an act of idolatry by all definitions of the term, especially when one considers that it was biblical proscription that abolished communal blood rituals and deemed human and animal sacrifice morally repugnant. Forty-four separate biblical prohibitions are violated in idolatry, and their gravity is underlined by the fact that martyrdom is enjoined before transgressing the idolatry laws. In addition to the obvious prohibitions concerning the worship of other gods, biblical proscription also forbids tattooing, self-mutilation, and ingesting blood. When artist Stembera drank a mixture of his own blood, urine, hair, and nail clippings in front of a self-made altar, and Journiac made a pudding with his own blood, they performed contemporary acts of idolatry. Biblical prohibitions on blood include, among others, the Levitical injunction to "eat no manner of blood, whether it be of fowl or of beast, in any of your dwellings. Whatsoever soul it be that eateth any manner of blood, even that soul shall be cut off from his people" (Lev. 7:26–27). In addition, "whatsoever man there be of the house of Israel, or of the strangers that sojourn among you, that eateth any manner of blood; I will even set my face against that soul that eateth blood, and will cut him off from among his people" (Lev. 17:10). When performance artist Bob Flanagan displays himself getting his nipples pierced, having his partner cut her initials into his chest, and with his own hands drives a nail through the head of his penis, one can confidently argue that this constitutes idolatry. The prohibition that is relevant to body mutilation as a form of art originally related to the practice of cutting oneself in a berievement practice, but it is certainly applicable to other forms of self-mutilation. In the *Mishneh Torah*, Moses Maimonides states: "Gashing and gouging oneself are governed by a single prohibition. Just as the pagans would gouge their flesh in grief over their dead, they would mutilate themselves for their idols, as [1 Kings 18:28] states: 'and they mutilated themselves according to their custom.' This is also forbidden by the Torah, as [Deut. 14:1] states: 'Do not mutilate yourselves.' "[15] When artist Ron Athey incorporates piercing, bloodletting, and tattooing in his performances to create rituals of redemption, he is practicing idol worship. In a 1993 performance titled "Martyrs and Saints," Athey hung nude, strung up to a column with long needles inserted into his head in such a manner as to represent a crown of thorns. His stated artistic intention was to achieve redemption through self-mutilation. Athey's whole body, including his face, is almost completely covered with tattoos. Maimonides states: "The tattooing which the Torah forbids involves making a cut in one's flesh and filling the slit with eye-color, ink, or with any other dye that leaves an imprint. This was the custom of the idolaters, who would make marks on their bodies for the sake of their idols."[16]

These are just a few examples of performances that conflict with biblical proscription. In *Saving the Appearances: A Study in Idolatry*, philosopher Owen Barfield provides a more useful definition for understanding the nature of violent expressions of the spiritual in performance art. He states:

In a wider frame of reference than that hitherto adopted, idolatry may be defined as the valuing of images or representations in the wrong way and for the wrong reasons; and an idol, as an image so valued. More particularly, idolatry is the effective tendency to abstract the sense-content from the whole representation and seek that for its own sake, transmuting the admired image into a desired object.[17]

This is initially similar to previous definitions; however, it differs with the addition of Barfield's concept of original participation which is especially pertinent to performance art. " 'Participation' begins by being an activity," he notes, "and essentially a communal or social activity." This activity occurs

> in rites and initiation ceremonies resulting in collective mental states of extreme emotional intensity, in which representation is as yet undifferentiated from the movements and actions which make the communion towards which it tends a reality to the group.

According to Barfield's theory, "participating cults naturally cluster about man-made images," and these will "evoke and focus the experience of nature as representation." He notes, for example, that a cluster of tress is "rendered more numinous by the idol in the grove," thereby connecting participation with idol worship. "Original participation," Barfield continues, "is the sense that there stands behind the phenomena, and on the other side of them from man, a represented, which is of the same nature as man. It was against this," he concludes, "that Israel's face was set. The devotee in the presence of the totem feels himself and the totem to be filled with the same 'mana.' They are both of them, 'stopping places for mana.' "[18] Barfield's concept of original participation points to the notion that idolatry consists not just in a representation of God or other gods but in the entire cultic sphere of image worship which includes ritual acts. Performance artists are trying to evoke the phenomenon of original participation to achieve a primal form of spirituality for themselves and sometimes for their audiences. They have gone beyond creating spiritual objects to becoming the spiritual object. Since the fundamental principle of the prohibition of idolatry is not to worship other gods or create objects of worship, biblical proscription is not only applicable to idols that consist of objects of wood and stone but also to artists who sculpt in their own blood and flesh. This explains why prohibitions on image-making are so essential to preserving monotheism that the Jewish sages declared that whoever transgressed the laws relating to idolatry was, as it were, transgressing the entire body of commandments of the Torah.

Body mutilation in contemporary art is often extremely violent and similar to another religious concept, mortification. In a wide variety of religious traditions, mortification occurs in the context of initiation rituals. Dario Sabbatucci notes: "The term mortification derives from the Latin *mortificare* ('to put to death')," and that "practices of mortification seem intended symbolically to assimilate the initiate into a deathlike condition that is to precede an initiatory rebirth."[19] The practices refer to specific forms of bodily discipline, ranging from sleep deprivation to ritual forms of abuse. Deprivations are ways of symbolizing death: the dead do not speak, eat, drink, or sleep. Violent rituals can be seen as endurance tests that serve as a rite of passage into adulthood. The significance is not the violent act but a symbolic death and rebirth. In Christianity mortification can be seen as an element in the more general practice of asceticism. The concept is derived from the Pauline ideal of participation in the crucifixion of Christ by putting to death the desires of the flesh. This self-imposed martyrdom was a way that Christians could recapture some of the self-sacrificing intensity of the early church. This included various degrees of self-inflicted violence, such as fasting, sleep deprivation, self-flagellation, or the wearing of what is referred to as a hair shirt—"a scourge worn as a belt against the naked flesh, the rope made more painful by being knotted or by the addition of metal nails."[20] The goal of this self-infliction of pain was to experience ecstatic union with God. In his book *Holy Anorexia*, Rudolph Bell describes the life of Catherine Benincasa, one of the many medieval women who tortured themselves as a form of Christian mortification:

> from the age of sixteen or so she subsisted on bread, water, and raw vegetables. She wore only rough wool and exchanged her hairshirt, the dirtiness of which offended her, for an iron chain bound so tightly against her hips that it inflamed her skin. For three years she observed a self-imposed vow of total silence except for confession . . . three times a day she flagellated herself with an iron chain . . . each beating lasted for one-and-one half hours and blood ran from her shoulders to her feet.[21]

"Catherine's religious devotions," notes Hewitt, "rewarded her with visions that led her to believe she experienced mystical union with God. She was canonized as a saint by the Catholic Church."[22]

In an interview with Andrea Juno and V. Vale in *Modern Primitives*, British performance artist Genesis P-Orridge recounts one of a series of art performances titled "Coum Transmissions" that has strikingly similar characteristics to mortification practices:

> Instinctively, without pre-planning, I started to do cuts—scrape my body with sharp nails (not razor blades; to me, that didn't feel ritualistic enough; it had to be a dagger or nail or implement) . . . I was pushing myself to the point of being declared near *dead*. At the last *Coum Transmissions* action in Antwerp . . . I started cutting a swastika shape into my chest about 9" square with a rusty nail; then I turned it into a Union Jack (the British Flag), and then just scratched and cut all over the place.[23]

After that performance he was rushed to the hospital where he had a near-death experience that included astral projection.

Another example of an art performance that exemplifies mortification practices is that of Sheree Rose and Bob Flanagan titled "Autopsy." Flanagan lies nude on an autopsy table while he is whipped, beaten, strangled, pinched with clothespins, has various objects inserted into his rectum, and has his penis sliced with a knife. The title has obvious references to death—Flanagan does not speak in this performance.[24]

The rationale behind both P-Orridge and Flanagan's art performances is that they are a means of achieving spiritual transformation through imposed or self-imposed pain and violence leading to deathlike conditions. The question remains, How does one distinguish this activity as performance art as opposed to simply an act of sadomasochism? In response to a similar question, P-Orridge stated:

> I've met genuine masochists and they're usually rather dull, because they don't give you any intellectual explanation at all, nor are they interested in one . . . I'm interested in *heightened awareness*, and I'm interested in learning more and more about—not just myself, but what is possible through the achievement of—not early trance states, but altered states in the true sense.[25]

This presents the conception of sadomasochism as a form of spiritual art, corresponding to the concept of mortification in initiation rituals and Christian asceticism.

Bataille, Girard, Eroticism, and Violence

It also corresponds to Georges Bataille's conception of sacrifice. In *Eroticism, Death and Sensuality,* he writes that it is "the common business of sacrifice to bring life and death into harmony, to give death the upsurge of life, life the momentousness and the vertigo of

death opening onto the unknown." He suggests a comparison between love and sacrifice:

> Both reveal the flesh. Sacrifice replaces the ordered life of the animal
> with a blind convulsion of its organs. So also with the erotic convulsion;
> it gives free rein to extravagant organs whose blind activity goes on be-
> yond the considered will of the lovers.[26]

Bataille's view of eroticism posits an interpretation of sadistic and
masochistic acts of lovemaking as a form of ritual sacrifice.

One example of what could easily be construed as masochism is
the work of French multimedia performance artist Orlan, who has
been undergoing a series of cosmetic operations as art performances. She incorporates religious imagery, food, and comments
on spirituality and its connection to the body while fresh blood is
running down her face and body. During her performances she re-
ceives liposuction and facial reconstruction while reading aloud and
eating. Her performance "Image/New Image(s) or the Re-incarna-
tion of Saint-Orlan" is intended to transform herself into a living
saint. Currently, Orlan has undergone nine separate operations
toward her physical transformation. She states: "It is no longer plas-
tic surgery, but revelation."[27] Orlan's ritualized surgeries are reminiscent of the mortification practices of the many medieval women
who tortured themselves to achieve spiritual ecstasy. This postmodern mortification further exemplifies the philosophy of Bataille,
who notes that "the urges of the flesh pass all bounds in the absence
of controlling will . . . If a taboo exists, it is a taboo on some elemen-
tal violence. This violence belongs to the flesh."[28] According to Bataille, the violent masochistic acts performed by P-Orridge, Flanagan, and Orlan are one means of achieving spiritual ecstasy through
the mutilation of the flesh, and these violent actions are prohibited
in Christian doctrine. There is no reason to doubt the artists' claims
that acts of self-mutilation and violence in their work provide personal transformations for them. However, the decision to practice
these violent rituals in the context of performance art, and then to
further complicate the matter with the intention to redeem or transform the audience, raises serious questions.

From both historical and religious perspectives, the use of self-mutilation in performance art fails as religious ritual and as ritual mortification because rites involving blood always require the participation of the group or community. When saints and monks performed

private individual rituals they had the full support of Christian ideology. When mortification occurs in the context of initiation rites, the ritual is part of an established cultural tradition. But artists do not have a collective doctrine of beliefs or a community of believers to support their rituals. In her book *Mutilating the Body: Identity in Blood and Ink*, Hewitt admits that "although those who inflict such alterations upon their bodies often ritualize the process and function within a supportive subcultural group, their actions are not true rituals because they are not part of a fully communally sanctioned and participatory experience, and they do not arise from longstanding cultural traditions."[29] This, however, is not the only reason why the use of blood in performance art does not succeed as religious ritual.

In *Violence and the Sacred*, French scholar René Girard proposes a concept he calls "the sacrificial crisis" which occurs when the entire sacrificial structure fails. According to this concept, rituals can fail when the sacrificial victim loses its mimetic relation with the community (creating a situation in which the sacrificial substitute is recognizably different from other members of the group), when there is an unequal balance between pure and impure violence, and when the rite is not believed in by the community. Furthermore, ritual failure can cause more harm and unleash even more uncontrollable violence. According to Girard, "anything that adversely affects the institution of sacrifice will ultimately pose a threat to the very basis of the community, to the principles on which its social harmony and equilibrium depend."[30] Violent performance art fails as ritual on all three counts and significantly represents the breakdown of Western culture as defined by Girard's concept. When performance artists use blood (their own or someone else's) that is HIV-positive, the act fails as a ritual because the blood itself is designated as "polluted" (in biblical terms). The sacrificial victims lose their mimetic relation to society because the artists are unacceptable surrogates or sacrificial victims for a healthy community. When performance artist Pane burns her feet and hands, gashes herself with a razor, and makes slits in her eyelids, the audience is not experiencing a sense of communal catharsis; indeed, it only serves to perpetuate a sense of horror at this vision of apparent inexplicable violence. As Girard argues:

> If the gap between the victim and the community is allowed to grow too wide, all similarity will be destroyed. The victim will no longer be capable of attracting the violent impulses to itself: the sacrifice will cease to serve as a "good conductor," in the sense that metal is a good conductor of electricity.[31]

Performance artist Athey (who is HIV-positive) caused a commotion when he pierced himself with needles, carved designs into an assistant's flesh, and then hung paper towels blotted with blood over the audience; members of the audience fled the auditorium in panic. This exemplifies Girard's concept of a sacrificial crisis; when the blood rite goes wrong, it only serves to set off a chain reaction of uncontrollable violence.

Many of the works cited above, specifically the more violent performances, are situated on the edge of mainstream American culture and are shocking even to veterans of the New York avant-garde art world. In order to gain a more complete understanding of the religious implications of the use of violence, mutilation, and blood in contemporary performance art, it is necessary to examine these works from the perspective of religious and societal censorship. Labeling violent performance art "the arts of disturbation," philosopher Arthur Danto notes:

> Reality must in some way be an actual component of disturbational art, and usually reality of a kind itself disturbing: obscenity, frontal nudity, blood, excrement, mutilation, real danger, actual pain, possible death . . . It is disturbation when the insulating boundaries between art and life are breached.[32]

According to Danto, disturbational art is a regressive movement; instead of going forward to its transfiguration into philosophy, it goes backward to the beginnings of art. The viewers' involvement with this art puts them in an entirely different frame of mind than anything for which the philosophy of art has equipped them. Danto proposes that:

> The disturbatory artist aims to transform her audience into something pretheatrical, a body which relates to her in some more magical and transformational relationship than the defining conventions of theater allow . . . the aim of the disturbatory artist is to sacrifice herself so that through her an audience may be transformed . . . it is an undertaking to recover a stage of art where art itself was almost like magic—like deep magic . . . in brief, it is an enterprise of restoring to art some of the magic purified out when art became art.[33]

The expression "when art became art" can be understood to mean when Jewish and Christian ideology vanquished this form of the aesthetic with biblical prohibitions on image worship. In his essay,

Danto suggests that disturbational art is what provoked the icono-
clastic controversies over the making of graven images at various
times in history:

> You after all have to ask yourself why there has been at various times in
> history such intense controversy over the making of graven images, why
> there have been movements of iconoclasm at all. It is a struggle against
> the use of dark powers on the part of artists who, by making an image of
> x actually capture x.[34]

Danto is describing the religious concept of idolatry. Self-mutilation,
specifically when the intention of the artist is spiritual redemption,
constitutes an idolatrous act because artists are substituting themselves for the idol or the scapegoat. The artist is becoming the other
god, and according to the biblical prohibition of images (as stated
in the Second Commandment), "Thou shalt have no other gods before me" (Exod. 20:3). Violent performance art will always be seen
as deviant in American society because self-mutilation, especially as
a form of sacrifice, cannot be culturally sanctioned in a society that
is founded on Jewish and Christian values.

Whereas an artist may achieve individual spiritual transformation
through his or her work, choosing to exhibit or perform publicly
entails viewer response and participation. When an artist posits himself as a sacrificial scapegoat during an art performance, the experience of the audience is determinedly meaningful in interpreting the
event. Interestingly enough, Danto's view of disturbatory art in aesthetics and Girard's theory of sacrifice in religion hold the same position with regard to the significance of audience participation. According to Danto, the viewer's choice of whether to participate in
a violent action or not is what distinguishes performance art from
anything the philosophy of art has prepared us to construe as art.
According to Girard, the viewer's choice of whether to participate
in a violent action or not is what distinguishes performance art from
acceptable ritual and ritual failure. So it is no coincidence that violent performance art does not fit into Danto's Hegelian construction of the history of art and, without audience participation, represents what Girard refers to as "a sacrificial crisis." In each case,
violent performance art is neither beneficial to, nor culturally sanctioned in, art or religion. This provides a nonbiblical explanation
for why the use of violence, mutilation, and blood in art is a secular
form of idolatry. It represents a struggle between those wishing to

retain the ethics and morality of a monotheistic society and those who believe in other ideologies. The principal point is that American art, religion, and culture cannot allow for self-mutilation and the use of blood in contemporary art for the same reasons that they are prohibited in the Bible: it is a threat to the fundamental principles of the Jewish and Christian worldview in which we live.

The fact remains that artists are increasingly using blood and violence in art and audiences are attending. This art can be referred to as "the art of idolatry" because it represents a spiritual attempt by artists to dismantle religious and societal boundaries through physical sacrifice as a form of religious ritual. Although this fails as religious ritual, it is ritual process nonetheless. Art is a mirror that reflects the soul of American culture, and however disturbing the idea may be, violence, self-mutilation, and the use of blood in contemporary performance art is revealing a strong need for ritual experience. This is even more apparent in the assimilation of these aesthetic expressions into popular culture as evidenced in the ritualization and acceptance of tattooing, piercing, branding, and body modifications. As Hewitt states:

> Self-starvation, self-cutting, performance art, and painful, permanent body adornment are . . . attempts to self-heal, self-initiate, and self-symbolize. In the context of culturally sanctioned rituals, these marks incur social inclusion and demarcate social status. In American society, which has considered body alteration practices barbaric and has few coming of age rituals that mark the body, the perception of these marks as deviant or perverse has been changing as they become more common.[35]

Body mutilation and decoration may begin as a mimicking of current trends. However, physical acts that permanently alter the body intrinsically alter conventional ideals of spirituality. Once assimilation of these violent expressions of the spiritual are culturally sanctioned, idolatry is achieved.

Notes

1. Howard Smagula, *Currents: Contemporary Directions in the Visual Arts* (Englewood Cliffs, N.J.: Prentice Hall, 1983), 222–23.

2. Roselee Goldberg, *Performance Art from Futurism to the Present* (New York: Abrams, 1988), 165.

3. Paul Schimmel, "Leap into the Void: Performance and the Object," *Out of*

Actions: Between Performance and the Object, 1949–1979 (New York: Thames & Hudson, 1998), 99.

4. Kristine Stiles, "Uncorrupted Joy: International Art Actions," *Out of Actions,* 304.

5. Hubert Klocker, "Gesture and the Object: Liberation as Aktion: A European Component of Performative Art," *Out of Actions,* 191.

6. Schimmel, "Leap into the Void," 84.

7. Goldberg, *Performance Art,* 164.

8. Stiles, "Uncorrupted Joy," 290.

9. Ibid., 293.

10. Kim Hewitt, *Mutilating the Body: Identity in Blood and Ink* (Bowling Green, Ohio: Bowling Green State University Press, 1997), 104. For a discussion of cannibalism, see the *Encyclopedia of Religion,* s.v. "cannibalism."

11. Hewitt, *Mutilating the Body,* 105.

12. V. Vale and Andrea Juno, eds., *Modern Primitives: An Investigation of Contemporary Adornment and Ritual* (San Francisco, Calif.: Re/Search Publications, 1989), 6.

13. *Encyclopedia of Religion,* s.v. "idolatry."

14. *Encyclopaedia Judaica,* s.v. "idolatry."

15. Moses Maimonides, *Mishneh Torah: The Laws of the Worship of Stars and Their Statutes,* trans. Eliyahu Touger (Jerusalem: Moznaim, 1990), 230.

16. Ibid., 226–28.

17. Owen Barfield, *Saving the Appearances: A Study in Idolatry,* 2d ed. (Middletown, Conn.: Wesleyan University Press, 1988), 110–11.

18. Ibid., 32, 110, 111.

19. *Encyclopedia of Religion,* s.v. "mortification."

20. Ibid.

21. Rudolph M. Bell, *Holy Anorexia* (Chicago: University of Chicago Press, 1985), 43.

22. Hewitt, *Mutilating the Body,* 45.

23. Vale and Juno, eds., *Modern Primitives,* 167, 168.

24. Ibid., 109–13.

25. Ibid., 169.

26. Georges Bataille, *Eroticism, Death and Sensuality* (1957), trans. Mary Dalwood (San Francisco, Calif.: City Lights Books, 1986), 92.

27. Linda Weintraub, Arthur Danto, and Thomas McEvilley, *Art on the Edge and Over: Searching for Art's Meaning in Contemporary Society, 1970s-1990s* (Litchfield, Conn.: Art Insights, 1996), 79.

28. Bataille, *Eroticism,* 92, 93.

29. Hewitt, *Mutilating the Body,* 100.

30. René Girard, *Violence and the Sacred,* trans. Patrick Gregory (Baltimore, Md.: The Johns Hopkins University Press, 1977), 49.

31. Ibid., 39.

32. Arthur C. Danto, *The Philosophical Disenfranchisement of Art* (New York: Columbia University Press, 1986), 121.

33. Ibid., 131,126.

34. Ibid., 127.

35. Hewitt, *Mutilating the Body,* 117–18.

Symbolic Politics:
Public Funding of the Arts

Matthew C. Moen
University of Maine

S OCIAL scientists have produced a vast literature in recent decades on the symbolic elements of politics. Many sociologists have argued that the rise of conservative political movements is a reaction to modernity and that public policy issues should be framed in terms of lifestyle defense.[1] Political scientists have focused on collective protest and the use of symbolic language in politics.[2] Drawing upon that literature, James Davison Hunter argued in the early 1990s that a "cultural war" was being waged by orthodox and progressive elements of our society.[3] He cited the arts as one battlefield in the culture war, where religious traditionalists and avantgarde artists fought intense battles over richly "symbolic territory."[4]

This essay uses the prism of symbolic politics to examine public funding for the National Endowment for the Arts (NEA). The annual legislative branch appropriation for the NEA is only a token amount of money in the annual federal budget: the president's recommendation for the NEA's FY 2001 budget, for instance, represented less than .00008% of the federal budget.[5] Yet, in spite of the modest sum of money, the NEA's budget has engendered fierce conflict over the years, suggesting that it is indeed a highly symbolic issue. That understanding makes even more sense when one realizes that mostly liberal Democrats have been the principal supporters of the NEA, while religiously conservative Republicans have been its principal opponents.

The Institutionalization of the NEA

The National Endowment for the Arts was created by Congress in 1965 as part of President Lyndon Johnson's Great Society. He argued that artistic achievement made available to all people was a hallmark of a civilized nation. Congressional supporters, such as Frank Thompson (Democrat, New Jersey), argued in complementary fashion that it was time "to make sure that our supply of humanists is large enough so that in future years machines remain the servant of mankind, and not vice versa."[6] The NEA whisked through the Senate by voice vote.

In contrast, the House of Representatives held some fierce opposition to the NEA. The conservative House Rules Committee initially refused to report the bill to the floor, and once it did, conservative Republicans and southern Democrats bitterly contested it. They advanced a number of different arguments.

Some of the arguments were fiscal in nature. Opponents said that $10 million split between the arts and humanities in FY '66 was excessive. They argued that federal support would discourage private donations to the arts and would encourage university faculty to feed at the public trough. They said the arts were a luxury, not a necessity, and that the money should be saved for other programs.

Opponents also pressed cultural arguments against creation of the NEA. Those arguments took radically different forms. One was that the arts were thriving in the United States, so public funding was superfluous. Opponents cited figures on the number of symphonies, museums, and libraries to prove their point.[7] Another (very different) argument was that federal support for the arts would undermine the artistic product by ensuring the survival of the mediocre artist who could not otherwise successfully compete in the marketplace. Simply put, public funding would facilitate the creation and dissemination of bad art.

Opposition to the NEA was confined to a minority of (House) members, but their determined efforts structured the final bill. Congress authorized $5 million for the NEA for three successive years. It also provided $5 million in matching funds, which was split fairly evenly between the NEA and state arts agencies. It gave $50,000 to every state art agency or a $25,000 grant for construction if a state lacked one. That formula dispersed the NEA monies to all states, thereby building support for the total package. It also decreased concern about the effects of federal funding on private patronage. Presumably, people would give more than ever to the arts since the federal government would match their contributions.

Once the initial struggle over the creation of the NEA was resolved, the agency encountered little trouble for many years. Elsewhere I have traced its regular legislative reauthorizations and its steadily increasing appropriations.[8] The same pattern repeated itself from 1968–1980. The sitting president of the day—Nixon, Ford, or Carter—routinely recommended an increase in the NEA's budget. The Senate usually accepted or even boosted the president's request, while the more frugal House settled on a lower figure. Supportive members on the House Education and Labor Committee and the Senate Labor and Public Welfare Committee sided with the NEA and the artistic community to create an influential "subgovernment." It won a 600% increase in agency appropriations over the course of the 1970s. Heading into the 1980s, support for the NEA was so strong that Congress passed authorizations with open-ended funding so that the inflation rate of the time could be taken into account when setting the NEA's final budget.

The situation changed under President Reagan. Delivering on a campaign pledge to challenge subgovernments in domestic policy areas, the administration proposed a 50% cut in the NEA's budget. The loss of important friends in Congress at that time compounded the NEA's problems. In response, Representative Fred Richardson (Democrat, New York) launched a Congressional Arts Caucus, which soon expanded to 150 members. While it could not fend off cuts, it reduced the proposed 50% cut to about 10% in FY '82 and FY '83. By FY '84, it helped win a modest budget increase. More importantly, the Arts Caucus won a record five-year reauthorization in 1985, ensuring that the NEA would outlast the Reagan Administration.[9]

Controversial Art

Although the NEA survived, it drew fire in the first year of the Bush administration (1989), when critics charged that it was subventing obscene projects. Controversy first erupted over an exhibit produced by artist Andres Serrano. He won a $15,000 prize from the Southeastern Center for Contemporary Art, and he used the funds to produce a number of works, including "Piss Christ." It was a reproduction of the Crucifixion submerged in a plastic container filled with the artist's urine. According to an art expert, it symbolized suffering and loss in life.[10] To religious conservatives, it was a malicious attack on their most sacred beliefs.

The Serrano exhibit caught the public eye when it was shown at

the Virginia Museum of Fine Arts. A self-described Christian fundamentalist sent a description of "Piss Christ" to Reverend Donald
Wildmon. He was an outspoken religious conservative from Tupelo,
Mississippi, who had spent much of the 1980s organizing boycotts of
offensive television programs through his group, the National Fed-
eration for Decency (the name was changed later to the American
Family Association, or AFA). In April 1989, Reverend Wildmon organized a massive letter-writing campaign to members of Congress.
Evangelical and fundamentalist Christians inundated Congress with
letters, postcards, and telephone calls, objecting to the Serrano exhibit. The campaign was wisely directed at NEA sponsorship of Serrano's work rather than at the Congress for funding the agency.
That allowed members of Congress to second-guess the NEA, arguing that an independent agency was failing to supervise its work.

On May 18, Senator Alphonse D'Amato (Republican, New York)
became the very first member of Congress to address the issue on
the floor. He denounced "Piss Christ" as a "deplorable, despicable
display of vulgarity," using phrases like "garbage, filth, and per-
verse" to describe it more fully.[11] D'Amato also submitted a letter to
Hugh Southern, Acting Chairperson of the NEA. It was signed by 23
senators, including liberals such as Tom Harkin (Democrat, Iowa)
and Bob Kerry (Democrat, Nebraska). The letter expressed outrage
over "Piss Christ" and called for a review of the NEA's grant-award-
ing procedures. Following its submission, Senator Jesse Helms (Republican, North Carolina) took to the floor where he called Serrano
a "jerk" and raised the spectre of abolishing the NEA entirely.

The uproar over "Piss Christ" might have ended quickly (it was
not covered by the *New York Times* or *Washington Post* in May 1989),
but a second NEA project quickly achieved notoriety. The Philadelphia Institute of Contemporary Art organized an exhibit of the work
of photographer Robert Mapplethorpe, with help of a $30,000 NEA
grant. Mapplethorpe had recently died of AIDS. The exhibit had
three controversial photographs. Two had homosexual themes,
while a third involved a naked child.

Controversy erupted when the Corcoran Gallery in Washington,
D.C. bowed to pressure from 100 House members, who wrote a letter demanding that Corcoran cancel its scheduled showing of Mapplethorpe's work. The cancellation placed the NEA on the national
stage. The *New York Times* and *Washington Post* ran nine stories each
in June 1989. Conservative Republicans and their allies in the Christian Right argued the exhibit was offensive. Democrats and liberal

Republicans noted that offensive works were only a small proportion of all NEA exhibits. They also focused on the fact that NEA sponsorship was indirect—through subcontracts to local arts agencies. The artistic community stressed the right to free expression in the First Amendment and that the money in question supported the exhibition of art, not its creation.[12] Artists rallied at the Corcoran Gallery to protest the decision to cancel the Mapplethorpe exhibit. Religious conservatives cared little whether tax dollars supported the creation or exhibition of art; they challenged the principle of public sponsorship, not the right of free expression.

Unfortunately for the NEA, its funding was contained in the Interior Appropriations bill, which was up for consideration in the House in July 1989. The timing was terrible for the NEA. The controversies immediately preceded congressional consideration of its budget. That sequence of events proved fortuitous for the set of conservative religious interest groups known as the Christian Right.

In Search of an Issue

The Christian Right arose in the late 1970s in reaction to theological challenges to religious orthodoxy and to numerous policy positions pushed by secular liberal actors.[13] The common theme for many fundamentalist and evangelical Christians is that their beliefs, values, and institutions were under attack. Their view was reinforced by federal government investigations into the tax-exempt status of conservative Christian schools.

During 1980 and 1984, leaders of the Christian Right worked to elect Ronald Reagan, registering hundreds of thousands of new voters.[14] During Reagan's first term, those leaders constructed a set of well-financed lobbies that pushed a set of social issues on Capitol Hill. Their major achievement was passage of an "equal access" bill that gave student religious groups access to public school facilities on the same basis as other student groups; the broader achievement was altering the congressional agenda.[15]

During the 99th Congress (1985–1986), the Christian Right underwent remarkable transformation. Many of its organizations—the National Christian Action Coalition, Religious Roundtable, the American Coalition for Traditional Values, Christian Voice, the Freedom Council—dissolved or atrophied. The premier group in the early

1980s (Moral Majority) was about to be merged into an umbrella organization to mask its declining membership.[16]

The wholesale organizational changes were one dimension of the Christian Right's transformation during that time. Other changes included: the erosion of a direct-mail base; the rise of Reverend Pat Robertson as titular leader of the Christian Right; a tactical reorientation away from Capitol Hill toward grass-roots activism; the substitution of the language of liberalism for the language of moralism; a decline in the Christian Right's public profile.[17] Ironically, the failures alienated supporters and the successes took the edge off their activism. Christian Right leaders spent much of the next two years reorganizing.

When George Bush took office in 1989, the Christian Right was in disarray. It basically consisted of three organizations: Concerned Women for America, which had moved from San Diego to Washington, D.C. in 1985; the American Freedom Coalition, a group supported by Reverend Sun Myung Moon; the Family Research Council, a group supported by Reverend James Dobson and headed by Gary Bauer, former domestic policy advisor to President Reagan. The latter groups were assembled in 1987 and 1988, respectively, and so they were just getting underway.

On the leadership front, Reverend Falwell had stepped back from politics to devote more time to his ministry and to Liberty University. Reverend Pat Robertson had unsuccessfully contested the 1988 Republican presidential nomination and was preoccupied with rebuilding his television ministry. The lessened visibility of those two men left the Christian Right without its preeminent leaders. It left an opportunity for Reverend Wildmon to lead the fight against the NEA.

Finally, and perhaps most seriously, the Christian Right was without a full and credible political agenda. In its early years, the movement had an abundant agenda. It struggled with the government over the tax-exempt status of its schools. It worked against the Equal Rights Amendment, pornography, and abortion. It was even on the cutting edge of certain issues, questioning the quality and content of the public schools and the use of the tax structure to drive familial arrangements.

Simply put, its agenda withered over the course of the 1980s. As one observer noted:

> In the early 1980s, its agenda was focused on the Equal Rights Amendment, abortion, and school prayer. Today, the ERA is a dead issue, which

was a victory for the movement. The school prayer issue is a dead issue also, which is a loss for the movement. With a couple of its major issues gone, the Christian Right has a pretty thin agenda.[18]

The same was true of tax-exempt schools and tuition tax credits—the Supreme Court stopped conservative Christian schools that practiced racial discrimination from having tax-exempt status, and high budget deficits killed tuition tax credits.

The Christian Right also stopped springing new issues in the 1980s, subordinating its own agenda to President Reagan's agenda. Christian Right leaders ambled into debates over the B-1 bomber, South African sanctions, budget and tax cuts, aid to the Nicaraguan resistance, and the Strategic Defense Initiative.

The emptiness of the Christian Right's agenda was obvious by 1987, when its leaders were reduced to marshaling support for Colonel Oliver North, who was involved in the Iran-Contra affair. He was invited to commencement at Liberty University and to the annual conventions of Concerned Women for America and the American Freedom Coalition.[19] In turn, Christian Right leaders raised money for his legal defense and collected petitions for a presidential pardon. The fact that the Christian Right spent so much time and effort on behalf of a single person involved in a political scandal rather than working to define American public life symbolized its thin agenda. The Christian Right looked for an issue like the NEA to regroup.

Much Commotion, Few Consequences

The fight on Capitol Hill differed in the House and Senate. The House focused on budget issues, while the Senate labored over content restrictions.

Opponents increased pressure on the NEA in the days leading up to the floor fight over the Interior appropriation, using the "one minute speeches" allowed under House rules to highlight the offensive works. On 12 July 1989, Sidney Yates (Democrat, Illinois)—chair of the Interior subcommittee with jurisdiction over the NEA's budget—tried to head off a floor fight by offering language requiring that subcontracted grants be personally approved by the NEA chairperson. Although the insertion of authorizing language into appropriations bills is done routinely, it is technically a violation of House rules. Dana Rohrabacher (Republican, California) objected, and he prevailed on the point of order.

Rohrabacher followed up with the suggestion to defund the NEA. It brought a sharp rebuke from several members. Les AuCoin (Democrat, Oregon) suggested that the Pentagon should be shut down if the House faithfully followed the logic that any waste in an agency should cause its abolition. AuCoin's point prompted a peculiar exchange about the virtues of cutting the NEA versus cutting one foot off American submarines, with the savings used to fund art. Sidney Yates said that Rohrabacher's proposal was like Ayatollah Khomeni's system of justice—too extreme. Paul Henry (Republican, Michigan) took the analogy further, saying that Rohrabacher's proposal was an "ayatollah amendment."[20]

The fallback position for NEA supporters was to rely on a favorable ordering of amendments by the House Rules Committee, consistent with its power to structure floor activity. The Rules Committee used a "king-of-the-hill" rule to protect the NEA from the conservative attack.[21] It ordered amendments in such fashion that the least draconian measure was considered first, followed by more severe amendments. The last measure to pass prevailed if more than one passed. Four amendments were ranked. The Stenholm Amendment cut $45,000 out of the NEA budget, a symbolic figure equal to the Serrano and Mapplethorpe awards. Other amendments cut 5%, 10%, and 100% of the NEA's budget, respectively. The key for NEA supporters was to pass the Stenholm Amendment, which let members "send a message" without inflicting much actual damage. The scheme worked.[22] The Stenholm Amendment passed by a 5 to 1 margin, with those opposing any cut in the NEA's budget siding with those who figured other measures would not pass and that a symbolic cut was better than nothing. Those in the middle also supported it as a reasonable option. Opposition came from two equally odd groups—liberals who opposed even a symbolic cut and conservatives who wanted to vote down the softest measure, gambling that they could win a tougher sanction. When the Stenholm amendment passed, it undercut support for harsher measures.

Religious conservatives were disappointed. They were helpless against legislative processes that worked against them, and they lost votes in spite of a massive letter-writing campaign and a television blitz against the NEA.

On the Senate side, Jesse Helms (Republican, North Carolina) attached language that restricted the types of projects eligible for

NEA funding. His amendment stopped the NEA from using funds to promote:

> obscene or indecent materials, including . . . depictions of sadomasoch-
> ism, homoeroticism, the exploitation of children, or individuals engaged
> in sex acts; material which denigrates the objects or beliefs of the adher-
> ents of a particular religion or non-religion; material which denigrates,
> debases, or reviles a person, group, or class of citizens on the basis of
> race, creed, sex, handicap, age, or national origin.[23]

It passed the Senate by voice vote at a time when only several members were present on the floor. The artistic community was livid. An
arts center in Phoenix displayed a work called "Piss Helms," which
had the senator's picture in a vat of beer.[24] The fate of Helms's language laid with House and Senate conferees.

During the conference committee negotiations, Senator Helms
tried to uphold content restrictions by having the Senate pass a reso-
lution instructing conferees to maintain that position. When he lost
that vote, conferees felt they could drop the language. They substi-
tuted much weaker language prohibiting the NEA from funding obscene projects, defined as lacking "serious literary, artistic, political,
or scientific value." That wording came from successive Supreme
Court decisions on obscenity. It was mostly symbolic since obscenity
is not a protected form of expression. Helms complained the language provided "a loophole so wide you can drive twelve Mack
trucks through it abreast."[25] In spite of the Serrano and Mapplethorpe exhibits, the NEA suffered only a $45,000 budget cut and
only symbolic content restrictions.

Funding in the 1990s

The cultural schism that erupted in 1989 became routinized in
the early 1990s. A few artists produced highly controversial works
with the assistance of NEA grants. The most offensive to religious
conservatives focused on lesbian and homosexual acts.[26] A minority
of House Republicans fought for budget cuts, but they had no real
success.[27] In fact, the NEA budget increased slightly in the early
1990s.

NEA supporters also fended off content restrictions. Those had
more broad-based support, especially in the Senate, but what hap-

pened several times is that restrictive language was dropped in a House and Senate conference committee. In 1991 identical restrictive language passed both chambers, prohibiting the NEA from funding projects that "promote, disseminate, or produce materials that depict or describe in a patently offensive way sexual or excretory activities or organs." It fell victim to a classic legislative deal over grazing fees for cattle, which meant more to Western senators than artistic restrictions.[28]

Yet, new projects kept up pressure on the NEA in 1993–1994. One called "Abject Art: Repulsion and Desire" included displays of dirt and rotten food. Particularly infuriating to members was a performance artist with AIDS who pricked himself and dangled a bloody towel over his audience on a clothesline. Even though the NEA's contribution to that performance was only about $150, many members considered it indefensible. They cut the NEA's budget by about 2% in 1994.[29]

When Republicans swept into power in the House and Senate in 1994 elections, the NEA's very existence was jeopardized. GOP leaders, such as Majority Leader Dick Armey (Republican, Texas) and Majority Whip Tom DeLay (Republican, Texas), favored abolishing the agency. Although they failed to kill the agency at their first opportunity, they rallied enough support to cut the NEA's budget from $162 million in FY '95 to $99 million in FY '96 (a 39% reduction). Moreover, they inserted language into the conference committee report that said the NEA should be abolished in two years.[30]

Two years later, during the fight over the FY '98 budget, the House finally zeroed out the NEA's budget. Described as some of the "fiercest fighting of the appropriations season," it began with an Appropriations subcommittee decision to give the NEA only $10 million for the coming year (a 90% reduction), mostly in the form of shutdown costs.[31] Yet even that figure was not realized. Following the scheme of Democrats in previous fights, Republican leaders used the Rules Committee to their advantage. They crafted a rule that headed off a straight up-or-down vote on the NEA's existence, on the grounds that its authorization had expired.[32] The rule passed on a 217–216 vote, following one unsuccessful attempt to redirect the NEA's budget directly to state art and education programs. The NEA survived only because the Senate refused to go along with the House action, appropriating nearly $100 million. In the conference committee, the Senate's position prevailed, and the NEA was funded at $98 million.

Subsequently, a threat from President Clinton to veto the relevant appropriations bill convinced many House Republicans to abandon their quest to kill the NEA. Some fifty-eight Republicans joined with virtually all House Democrats to fund the NEA at $98 million in FY '99. That total was much less than the $136 million sought by President Clinton, but it closely mirrored the Senate figure. After the vote, NEA Chairperson William Ivey said: "The old debate over the existence of the NEA finally has given way to a more thoughtful dialogue about the appropriate level of federal arts funding in America."[33] His comment was borne out in the next year, as Congress agreed to similar funding levels for the NEA in FY 2000. At the end of the 1990s, the NEA was still in existence, while the social conservatives who had pushed for its abolition were once again in disarray.[34]

Looking back, the NEA survived the funding battles and the content restrictions that first started in 1989 over the work of Andres Serrano and Robert Mapplethorpe. Yet, the NEA has not emerged unscathed. It has received intense congressional scrutiny for more than a decade. Its reauthorizations have been regularly shortened.[35] Its appropriations have been flat each year since Republicans gained control of Congress and only at about the level that the agency was receiving back in the mid-1970s (minus inflationary losses). Proposals to redirect its budget and limit its discretion now have been considered many times in Congress.

Arts and Politics in the New Millennium

There is nothing intrinsic about public funding of the arts that creates conflict with religion. Some of the most famous art in history has been sponsored by the regime or religious patrons, and much of it is respectful toward religion. Likewise, there is nothing intrinsic with the NEA that causes confrontation with religious conservatives. Since the NEA was launched in 1965, it has sponsored more than 111,000 projects.[36] Its conventional grant supports a symphony, dance, painting, or play that has little to do with religion. Only a fraction of NEA projects have offended religious conservatives and then only in recent years.

A contributing factor is that some artists seem to go out of their way to offend religious conservatives. Doing so pushes the bounds of artistic freedom and defies the statutory limits crafted by legislators. For their part, religious conservatives seem to go out of their way to inflate issues out of their proper context. They seem to do so in calculated fashion to reinvigorate a social movement that is sputtering at the beginning of the new millenium.[37]

The work of David Wojnarowicz illustrates these points. He produced an exhibit called "Tongues of Flame" with the help of a $15,000 NEA grant. Displayed at Illinois State University, it had a painting of Christ with a syringe in his arm, suggesting drug addiction.[38] That deliberate provocation caught the attention of Reverend Don Wildmon, who used it as a conduit for raising money. In turn, Wojnarowicz brought suit against Wildmon. He noted that the portrayal of Christ with a syringe in his arm was about 2.5% of a 6 x 8 foot painting, arguing that Wildmon's reproduction of that portion of the painting in a fundraising letter was entirely out of context. That controversy typifies the political struggle and symbolizes the cultural divide between artists and religious conservatives in contemporary times.

The NEA is likely to remain in the public eye. As a quasi-independent government agency, it must receive periodic reauthorization and an annual appropriation. The routine and predictable cycle invites regular conflict, even if the intensity abates at times. Ironically, earlier efforts by NEA opponents have probably aided the agency in recent years. When religious conservatives first tried to rally support against the NEA, one line of their reasoning was that NEA funding went disproportionately to "arts states," such as California and New York. Why should Alabama or South Dakota taxpayers support artistic exhibits in Los Angeles or Manhattan, they asked? Members of Congress listened—and they increased the proportion of NEA funds distributed to state arts agencies.[39] The effect was to build a stronger base of political support for the NEA by distributing its benefits more liberally across congressional districts.

President Clinton's proposal to increase support for the arts through the "Challenge America" program is an extension of that tactic. Clinton proposed to increase funding for the NEA by about $50 million to a level of $150 million in FY 2001 (about a 30% increase from FY 2000 levels). Interestingly, the Challenge America program favors geographic dispersion of benefits, a pork-barrel technique proven effective in legislatures.[40] The program would fund 1000 small art project grants in targeted communities, 150 grants to arts organizations around the country, and some 20 national initiatives involving cooperation with federal agencies and nonprofit organizations. About 40% of the funds would be directed to state arts agencies.[41] Although Clinton's proposal was smart politics, it also symbolizes the genuine difficulties the NEA faces even today, more than a decade after Andres Serrano caught the attention of religious conservatives. NEA supporters believe they must resort to devolution and geographic dispersion to win budgetary increases.

The NEA seems destined to enjoy a long life of ill health. For the foreseeable future, it will remain what it has been for more than a decade—a symbol of a cultural divide that shrinks and expands at different times, but does not go away.

Notes

1. For example, Joseph Gusfield, *Symbolic Crusade: Status Politics and the American Temperance Movement* (Urbana: University of Illinois Press, 1963); Seymour Martin Lipset and Earl Rabb, *The Politics of Unreason* (New York: Harper & Row, 1970). A good review of this literature is Clyde Wilcox, *God's Warriors* (Baltimore, Md.: The Johns Hopkins University Press, 1992), 27–40.

2. Murray Edelman, *The Symbolic Uses of Politics* (Urbana: University of Illinois Press, 1970); Murray Edelman, *Politics as Symbolic Action* (New York: Academic Press, 1971).

3. James Davison Hunter, *Culture Wars: The Struggle to Define America* (New York: Basic Books, 1991).

4. Ibid., 230–49.

5. For additional information on Clinton's FY 2001 request, see the Web page of the National Endowment for the Arts, <http://www.arts.gov>.

6. *Congressional Record,* 13 September 1965, 23619.

7. "Foundation on the Arts and Humanities," *1965 CQ Almanac* (Washington: Congressional Quarterly Press, 1966), 621–27.

8. Matthew C. Moen, "Congress and the National Endowment for the Arts: Institutional Patterns and Arts Funding, 1965–1994," *Social Science Journal* 34, no. 2 (1997): 186–200.

9. "Arts, Humanities Funding," *1985 CQ Almanac* (Washington: Congressional Quarterly Press, 1996), 293.

10. Peggy Phelen, "The First Amendment and Public Support of the Arts," roundtable at the Annual Meeting of the American Political Science Association, Washington, D.C., September 1991.

11. *Congressional Record,* 18 May 1989, S5594.

12. Phelen, "The First Amendment."

13. Kenneth D. Wald, *Religion and Politics in the United States,* 3d ed. (Washington: Congressional Quarterly Press, 1997), 217–66.

14. For a good summary of an extensive literature estimating evangelical voter turnout in the early 1980s, see Corwin Smidt, "Evangelicals and the 1984 Election," *American Politics Quarterly* 15 (1987): 419–44.

15. Matthew C. Moen, *The Christian Right and Congress* (Tuscaloosa: University of Alabama Press, 1989), 141–47.

16. Robert Pear, "Falwell Forming Group to Look at Broad Issues," *New York Times*, 4 January 1986, 5.

17. Matthew C. Moen, *The Transformation of the Christian Right* (Tuscaloosa: University of Alabama Press, 1992); see also Mark J. Rozell and Clyde Wilcox, *Second Coming: The New Christian Right in Virginia Politics* (Baltimore, Md.: The Johns Hopkins University Press, 1996).

18. Interview with Michael Schwartz, Free Congress Foundation, 16 October 1989.

19. "North Says Criminal Charges Against Him Are an Honor," *New York Times*, 3 May 1988; Henry Mohr, "End Ollie's Persecution Now, Mr. President," *American Freedom Journal* (December 1988/January 1989), 5–7.

20. *Congressional Record*, 12 July 1989, H3639–3642.

21. On innovative rules, see Stanley Bach and Steven S. Smith, *Managing Uncertainty in the House of Representatives: Adaptation and Innovation in Special Rules* (Washington: Brookings Institution, 1988).

22. Moen, "Congress and the National Endowment for the Arts," 192–93.

23. "The Helms Process," *New York Times*, 28 July 1989, 26.

24. Miriam Horn and Andy Plattner, "Should Congress Censor Art?" *U.S. News and World Report*, 25 September 1989, 22–24.

25. See "Language on Obscene Art Hangs Up Interior Bill," *1989 CQ Almanac* (Washington: Congressional Quarterly Press, 1990), 731–37.

26. George Archibald, "Sexual Performers Tucked Into List for New NEA Grants," *Washington Times*, 1 January 1991; Allan Parachini, "Conservative Group Renews Attack on NEA," *Los Angeles Times*, 27 March 1991.

27. One victory for religious conservatives was that NEA Chairperson John Frohnmayer was ousted by President George Bush as one way of deflecting the primary challenge of rival Patrick Buchanan in the 1992 election.

28. Moen, "Congress and the National Endowment for the Arts," 197.

29. "Interior Bill Wins Easy Passage," *1994 CQ Almanac* (Washington: Congressional Quarterly Press, 1995), 515–16.

30. "President Rejects Interior Bill," *1995 CQ Almanac* (Washington: Congressional Quarterly Press, 1996), 11–48 to 11–54.

31. "Interior Bill Dodges Controversies," *1997 CQ Almanac* (Washington: Congressional Quarterly Press, 1998), 9–44 to 9–49.

32. Ibid., 9–46.

33. "Funding Increased, Host of GOP Riders Fall in $14.1 Billion Interior Bill," *1998 CQ Almanac* (Washington: Congressional Quarterly Press, 1999), 2–60.

34. Dan Carney, "Conservative Culture War Pauses for a Reality Check," *Congressional Quarterly Weekly Report*, 27 March 1999, 738–43.

35. Moen, "Congress and the National Endowment for the Arts," 197.

36. National Endowment for the Arts Web page, <http://www.arts.gov>.

37. John C. Green, Mark J. Rozell, and Clyde Wilcox, eds., *Prayers in the Precincts: The Christian Right in the 1998 Elections* (Washington: Georgetown University Press, 2000).

38. Kim Masters, "Artist Sues Anti-NEA Group for Use of His Work," *Washington Post*, 22 May 1990, C1–2.

39. For background on NEA allocations, see Edward Arian, *The Unfilled Promise: Public Subsidy of the Arts in America* (Philadelphia, Penna.: Temple University Press, 1989).

40. R. Douglas Arnold, *The Logic of Congressional Action* (New Haven, Conn.: Yale University Press, 1990).

41. "Challenge America: A Proposal for FY 2001 to Strengthen Communities Through the Arts," National Endowment for the Arts Web page, <http://www.arts.gov/learn/facts/challenge2.html>.